THE WOOLLEN INDUSTRY

University for the Creative Arts

Item Title	Due Date
* British sheep and wool	01/04/2019
* Living in Norway	01/04/2019
* Interior inspiration : Scandinavia	01/04/2019
* The woollen industry : an outline of the woollen industry and its processes from fibre to fabric	01/04/2019
* Contemporary textile art : Scandinavia	01/04/2019
* From Scandinavia : graphic design from Scandinavia	01/04/2019

* Indicates items borrowed today
Thank you for using self-service.

THE
WOOLLEN INDUSTRY

An outline of the woollen industry and its
processes from fibre to fabric

by
ALAN BREARLEY
BSc, CText, FTI, FBIM, FIMA, CGIA

Formerly Vice-Principal, Dewsbury and
Batley Technical and Art College

and
JOHN A. IREDALE
TD, MBA, PhD, CText, FTI

Lecturer in Spinning Technology
University of Bradford

Published by Wira, the research and services centre
for textiles, carpets and clothing

1st edition © 1965 Alan Brearley
2nd edition © 1977 Alan Brearley and John A. Iredale
2nd impression 1981

ISBN 0 900820 10 1

*Front cover photograph shows a modern woollen carding
and spinning installation. Reproduced by permission of
J.B. Battye & Co Ltd, a member of the Readicut Group.*

Published by Wira, Wira House, West Park Ring Road, Leeds, LS16 6QL

Printed in Great Britain by Wira, Leeds and
Thornton & Pearson (Printers) Ltd, Bradford

Preface

Stocks of the first edition of *The Woollen Industry* (written by Alan Brearley and published by Pitman in 1965) were exhausted in 1974. As a result of many enquiries received from students, colleges and libraries both in the UK and overseas, it became obvious that a second edition was urgently required. Wira offered to undertake the printing, publishing and distribution, so in order to effect a quick, yet complete, revision of the book, the previous author enlisted the assistance of Dr John A. Iredale, a friend for many years and one-time colleague at Wira (then the Wool Industries Research Association). It is to Dr Iredale that much of the credit is due for up-dating the text and providing new photographs and diagrams where these were deemed necessary.

The aim of the second edition of *The Woollen Industry* is essentially the same as for the first edition; that is, to provide in easily readable form information covering the whole range of operations involved in the production of woollen yarn and cloth. A brief account is also given of the history, growth, development and organization of the woollen industry. The reader is shown the interdependence of one operation on another and special emphasis is laid on the principles of processing. To describe the complex details of all the machinery used in converting fleece-wool and other textile raw materials into woollen fabrics would have necessitated a much bulkier volume, so a Bibliography has been included near the end of the book and the reader can consult those references for more detailed information on specific machines or processes.

Care has been taken to make the manner of presentation interesting, and *The Woollen Industry* is illustrated with numerous diagrams and photographs showing a representative selection of the machinery and processes currently in use in the woollen industry. At the same time the latest trends, and major developments which have found successful application in industry, have been included and critically assessed in their respective places throughout the text. Metric units are used extensively, but since imperial units are still often employed in practice these are given also.

It is hoped that *The Woollen Industry,* like its companion volume *Worsted* (originally published in 1964 and shortly to be produced as a second revised edition by Alan Brearley and John A. Iredale and published by Wira) will be of use to students, trainees and apprentices in the textile trade, and also to young people about to enter the industry. Teachers in junior, secondary and comprehensive schools and in colleges of further and higher education may find the book helpful as a source of information on one of the UK's most important industries. *The Woollen Industry* could well be of assistance to students in other branches of the textile industry who are preparing for the Textile Institute's Associateship examinations, as well as to people engaged in the distributive trades, where a knowledge of how the constituents of an article of woollen clothing are made can be of inestimable value.

The authors gratefully acknowledge the help of many machinery makers, mill managements and other organizations who have taken so much trouble to provide photographs to illustrate specific points in the text. At the same time they apologize to those firms whose products have not been included, and trust that they will appreciate that space does not permit descriptions of all possible versions of the machinery now available to the woollen industry.

Advice has been received from many sources, but thanks are especially due to several members of the staff of Wira, particularly Mr Frank G. Lambert, head of Site Services, Mr R.T. Dennis Richards of the woollen department, and Mr Rollo Bruce, editor. The authors are also grateful to many associates, past and present, who directly or indirectly have influenced the writing of this book.

ALAN BREARLEY
JOHN A. IREDALE

Halifax, January 1977

Contents

List of Advertisers

CHAPTER 1

Woollen and Worsted

Garments made from wool may be either woollens or worsteds. The difference between these two classes of goods is not usually understood by people who are not intimately connected with the trade. Quite often a certain article of clothing which is labelled *all wool* may be incorrectly referred to by the layman as *woollen,* whereas in reality the particular garment should be more correctly termed *worsted.* It is hoped that the following explanations will help to clear up any confusion that may exist in the reader's mind.

Woven fabrics are made from yarns, which in turn are composed of textile fibres twisted together. The *basic* fibre used for both woollen and worsted goods is wool, but in worsted yarns the fibres have been laid parallel to each other during manufacture giving the yarn and the ultimate fabric a neat, smooth appearance, whereas yarns in which the fibres are crossed in all directions and are not parallel, and therefore have a rough, whiskery appearance, are woollen. Cloth is named after the yarns that compose it, and Plates 1 and 2 show photographs of woollen and worsted yarns and fabrics. The woollen cloths appear full-handling and bulky, but the worsted fabrics have a clear, smooth, regular surface with the individuality of each thread apparent in the pattern of the weave.

THE NAMES 'WOOLLEN' AND 'WORSTED'

Woollen is a clear enough term to the layman and signifies something to do with wool, but it is doubtful whether many people, even some workers in the industry, could say much about the derivation of the term worsted.

Worsted is a slight corruption of *Worstead,* the name of a village in Norfolk. It was here that the expert cloth workers who entered England in the early fourteenth century as refugees from religious and political tyranny on the Continent, particularly from Flanders, first settled and introduced 'new and original' methods for the production of superior and finer cloth than had hitherto been made in Britain. Formerly a flourishing town, Worstead is now an agricultural village without an industrial spindle or loom.

DIFFERENCES IN RAW MATERIALS

Only virgin wool is used in *worsted* manufacture*. In order to make a yarn with
a clear outline the worsted trade uses wool fibres which have been combed. This
process straightens the longer fibres and removes the shorter ones. All worsted
yarns, except a small percentage used for making carpets and some hand knitting
wools, are made from combed wool; in the manufacture of worsted-spun carpet
yarn the combing process is sometimes omitted for economy and also to leave in
the yarn the short fibres which contribute to the *lift* of the finished carpet. This
system may be referred to as Semi-Worsted. All the machines used in worsted
yarn manufacture help to maintain the smoothness of the thread.

The *woollen* spinner may use virgin wool also, but on the other hand his yarns
may not contain any *new* wool at all, for in addition to pure wool he has at his
disposal a wide variety of other fibrous materials including—

(a) shoddy—fibrous material produced by tearing up old and new knitted
garments or loosely-woven fabrics in rag form,

(b) mungo—produced in a similar way to shoddy but the rags used
comprise new or old hard-woven or milled† cloth or felt,

(c) noils—these are pure wool of short fibre length removed from the
longer wool fibres during the combing process in worsted yarn
manufacture,

(d) cotton, rayon and other man-made fibres in the staple form,

(e) wastes made at various stages of textile processing.

These materials will be considered in more detail in Chapter 5. Wools of short
fibre length can be used in the woollen industry—indeed it is said that the low
woollen trade can deal with any fibre, however short, so long as it has two ends!
Short wools which lack sufficient length for combing are often termed *clothing
wools* and are used for woollens, whereas wools which are classed as suitable in
length for the combing process and used in the worsted industry are termed
combing wools.

DIFFERENCES IN PROCESSING WOOLLENS AND WORSTEDS

There are many more worsted than woollen processes, and it is probably true to
say that in yarn manufacture it may require almost as many weeks to pass from
raw material to yarn in worsted processing as it requires hours in woollen
manufacture.

---

*When man-made fibres are processed on worsted or woollen machinery the yarn should be
referred to as worsted-spun or woollen-spun respectively and not merely worsted or woollen.

†See Chapter 14.

To produce a woollen yarn the components of the blend are first mixed together in *blending* machinery. The resultant blend is then processed into *slubbings* on a woollen carding machine, and finally the slubbings are spun into yarn on a woollen mule or a woollen spinning frame. In worsted yarn manufacturing, however, after the wool has been scoured and dried it is usually carded. It must then be combed and gilled, followed by a series of drawing operations before it is finally spun*. At every stage attempts are made to lay the fibres parallel to each other in order finally to produce a smooth worsted yarn. There may be as many as twenty machines in the sequence of operations for worsted yarn as against only three or four for a woollen yarn.

After weaving there are many more possibilities in the range of *finishes* which can be applied to woollens than to worsteds. In fact it has been said that 'a worsted cloth is made in the loom whereas a woollen cloth is made in the finishing't. Usually there is little difference in general appearance between a *worsted* cloth taken from the loom and the same fabric ready for dispatch to the customer, but seldom can the same be said of a *woollen* fabric. Indeed a woollen blanket as it comes from the loom looks bare and thready, whereas on sale in the shop it is a fibrous, soft-handling article, and all this is due to the finishing processes.

---

*For a complete account of worsted processing the reader is referred to Worsted by Alan Brearley, published by Pitman (1964), shortly to be republished by Wira in revised form.

†This is not entirely true. The real difference is in the yarn, but cloth finishing can alter the appearance.

CHAPTER 2

Early History, Growth and Development of the Woollen Industry

A full account of the history of the wool textile trade would fill a book itself and it is only possible to give here a brief outline of the milestones in the growth of the woollen industry from the earliest days of civilization to the present time. As will be seen, the *woollen* trade cannot be entirely divorced from the other branches of the textile industry, especially worsted and cotton.

THE EARLIEST METHODS OF SPINNING*
Archaeologists tell us that sheep already existed when man made his first appearance on earth, and there seems little doubt that wool was one of the earliest textile fibres available for spinning into yarn and weaving into cloth. We conjecture that our early ancestors first twisted a few fibres from a lock of wool into a short length of yarn and then extended this into a longer continuous length. Probably two people worked together, one spinning whilst the other would wind the yarn thus produced into a ball. Indeed some African tribes use this method today for cotton.

At a later period a stick was used on to which the yarn was wound, and from this there developed a method whereby the stick was made to do the twisting of the fibres into a yarn by turning it between the fingers. Later a fly-wheel was added to the lower end of the stick (Fig.1 (i)). Large quantities of these *spindle whorls* have been found in remains dating from about 2000 B.C. The spinning action produces a worsted-type yarn (*see* Chapter 1) but includes *all* the fibres, short and long, when spinning is done from a lock of wool. This simple spindle was used for spinning wool in Babylon, Greece and Rome, cotton in India, and flax in Egypt. Homer (*c.* 900 B.C.) tells us that Helen of Troy used such a spindle, and a golden distaff for holding the wool, whilst Herodotus (484–425 B.C.) wrote of a girl in Lydia who 'returned, carrying a pitcher of water on her head, leading a horse and *turning her spindle'*.

*Much of the information on the history of spinning is due to the late Commander Hugo Lemon, at one time Editor at Wira, whose help on this topic in the first edition the authors gratefully acknowledge; also Fig. 1 (iii).

HAND CARDING FOR WOOLLENS

The Romans evidently used some form of carding (*see* Chapter 9) for teasing out the wool in preparation for spinning. Ovid (43 B.C.–A.D. 17) tells that Arachne carded wool before spinning it. It can be assumed that the earliest hand cards were somewhat similar to those used by *hand* spinners today (*see* Fig. 1 (ii)), but instead of steel pins, teazles were used. The Latin for thistle is *carduus* and this is obviously how the term *carding* originated. Hand carding was the only method available up to the mid-eighteenth century when machines were invented for doing the work*.

*Carding engines as we know them today were not used until well into the nineteenth century. (See Chapter 9.)

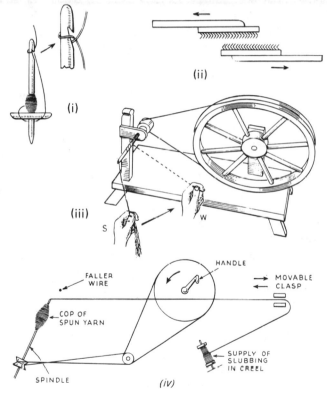

(i) Simple suspended spindle.
(ii) Hand cards.
(iii) One-thread or Great Wheel (S-hand in the *spinning* position; W-hand is *winding* the spun yarn on to the spindle to form a cop).
(iv) Spinning Jenny. (For further details of (iii) and (iv) *see* the Bibliography.)

FIG. 1 Historical aspects of woollen spinning

HAND COMBING FOR WORSTED

Although our account is concerned chiefly with woollens, at this juncture we must digress for a few lines and consider worsted processing. In place of carding a better way of preparing wool for *worsted*-type yarns was found to be combing. Indeed carding was not used for worsteds until the middle of the nineteenth century. The early history of combing is obscure, as it is for carding. It is known that the Romans used combs, wooden pronged implements, for beating up the weft in weaving (*see* Chapter 13), for preparing wool for spinning and for combing the fleeces on their sheep.

Some form of hand combing was certainly practised in England in the early Middle Ages and was used as one of the stages in *worsted* processing from then until the middle of the nineteenth century. Methods of combing varied at different periods and in different localities. The *top* (a ball of combed sliver) which was produced by combing went to the spinster for hand spinning in the earlier days, and to worsted drawing machines in later times.

SPINNING WHEELS

We now go back a few hundred years to take up the story of the actual spinning operation once more. The simple spindle continued to provide the *only* method of spinning in Europe until about A.D. 1300, and it was commonly used for a long time after that. The first spinning wheel used in Europe worked on the same principle as the *Charkha* from India. In Europe it developed in about the fourteenth century into the *Great Wheel,* also known as the *Welsh* or *One-thread Wheel* (Fig. 3 (iii)), or in Scotland as the *Muckle Wheel.* It was eminently suitable for cotton and for spinning *short* wools into *woollen* yarn and it was also used for spinning combed wool slivers (*see* above) into *worsted* yarn; it was the direct ancestor of—

1. Hargreaves' Spinning Jenny, (Fig. 1 (iv)),
2. Crompton's Mule,
3. Roberts' Self-acting Mule,
4. The Woollen Mule of today,

all of which are explained later.

Thus in Europe in the early Middle Ages two methods of spinning were available—

1. The simple spindle with *worsted* action,
2. The one-thread wheel with *woollen* action.

In addition there was a crude form of hand combing for preparing wool for *worsted* spinning, and hand carding for *woollen* spinning.

As a matter of interest it can be noted here that in about 1500 Leonardo da Vinci set down clearly in drawings the principle of what was later to be known as the Saxony or Flax Wheel. This was intended essentially for *worsted*-type yarns. In about 1555 it was first used in Saxony and the credit was given to Johann Jürgen, believed to be either a wood-carver or a stone-mason of Wolfenbüttel, near Brunswick. There does not appear to be any evidence, however, that this type of wheel was used much in Britain before 1800.

EARLY METHODS OF CLOTH MANUFACTURE

The first loom is thought to have been a straight branch of a tree, reasonably parallel to the ground. The threads which were to form the *warp (see* Chapter 13) were hung from this, and were weighted by stones or clay at their lower ends. Another thread (today known as the *weft)* was interlaced with the warp threads to form a rough cloth. Later the branch was replaced by a framework, and such vertical looms were used by the ancient Greeks. The loom was later made horizontal as it is today (*see* Chapter 13). The ancient Egyptians used both horizontal and vertical looms and they are given the credit for inventing the shuttle to hold the weft, and also for tying the warp threads to two sticks for the purpose of parting the threads so that the shuttle of weft could be passed through them.

From time to time improvements were made to the loom, such as the fitting of foot-treadles to move the warp threads so that the weaver's hands were free to work the shuttle of weft; but for weaving wide cloths two weavers were needed, one at each side of the loom, to throw the shuttle across. In 1733 John Kay of Bury introduced his *flying shuttle* which enabled much wider cloths to be made by one weaver working alone, and at speeds much faster than before; whilst Robert Kay's drop-box loom invented in 1760 made possible the use of more than one shuttle (*see* Chapter 13). In 1785—6 many of the previous ideas were incorporated in the first *power loom* made by Dr Edmund Cartwright, a clergyman. It is said to have been driven first by an ox and then by water power. (Incidentally it was the same Dr Cartwright who, from about 1790 to 1800, did the pioneering work on wool combing, which paved the way in the worsted industry for the machine-comb inventors of the mid nineteenth century.)

MECHANIZATION OF SPINNING

The introduction of Kay's flying shuttle speeded up the weaving process and therefore increased the demand for yarn to such as extent that it could not be met by the existing hand spinning wheels with their single spindles. In 1764 James Hargreaves (a Lancashire cotton weaver) started work on his *Spinning Jenny.* First it was used for cotton and had eight spindles on one machine (Fig. 1 (iv)). The Jenny was finally patented in 1770 and spun sixteen threads at once on the woollen principle. The yarn produced was good but not strong enough for warp, so warp yarns were spun on the *worsted* principle on a machine called a *Water Frame* (invented by Arkwright about 1769), so named because it was driven by water power. Whereas Hargreaves had mechanized the One-thread Wheel and patented his Jenny, Richard Arkwright of Preston mechanized the Saxony Wheel and in his Water Frame of 1769 he substituted two pairs of rollers (one pair rotating faster than the other) for the two hands of the spinster. His first machine had four flyers and spindles   and was essentially a machine working on the *worsted* principle. It was first used for cotton and later for worsted yarns.

Other spinning inventions followed rapidly. In 1779 Samuel Crompton, a spinner who lived near Bolton invented his *mule,* so named because it was a cross between the principles employed in Hargreaves' Spinning Jenny and Arkwright's Water Frame. This machine could draw out the fibres, twist them into a yarn and wind many threads on to the spindles at the same time. It was used first for cotton and subsequently for worsted, and was later adapted for woollen spinning. A great step forward took place in 1825 when Roberts made the woollen mule *self-acting,* and the machine has changed little in principle up to the present day.

Around 1830 the ring spinning frame was invented in the U.S.A. for cotton and worsted yarns, but it was not until the early twentieth century that the principle was first tried for producing woollen yarns and then only to a very limited extent. However in recent years this method has in many areas largely replaced the mule (*see* Chapter 10).

The development of spinning machinery is summarized in Table 1.

THE 'DOMESTIC SYSTEM'
The early fourteenth century has already been mentioned (page 1) as the time when the *worsted* industry first started in Britain. At that time woollen-type fabrics were being made all over the country by people in their own homes (hence the term *homespun),* and this domestic system continued until the early nineteenth century. Often farming and the wool industry were found together, changing places according to the time of the year. When the weather held up farming, its place was taken by weaving.

Cloth production was essentially a family affair, especially in the West Riding of Yorkshire, where the wife and daughters spun the wool yarn while the men combed the wool (for *worsted yarns)* and also wove the yarn into fabric. Then the weaver carried his woollen cloth to the local *fulling* mill to be scoured and *fulled.* The latter operation originally consisted in treading on the damp cloth to consolidate it (hence the name *Walker).* The modern name for this process which since the early Middle Ages has been carried out by some kind of machinery is *milling.* Fulling stocks were occasionally found in the late twelfth century but were not common until the fourteenth, whilst the rotary milling machine was not used until about 1833. (The West of England became famous for its thick, milled woollen cloth). After fulling, the cloth was dried by air on a wooden frame called a *tenter** usually in a field adjoining the weaver's home. Tentering machines using heated air were not developed until the mid-nineteenth century†.

TABLE 1
Development of Spinning Machines (Woollen and Worsted)

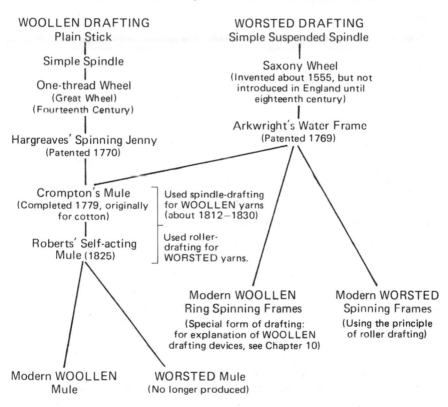

WOOLLEN DRAFTING
Plain Stick
Simple Spindle
One-thread Wheel
(Great Wheel)
(Fourteenth Century)
Hargreaves' Spinning Jenny
(Patented 1770)
Crompton's Mule
(Completed 1779, originally for cotton)
Roberts' Self-acting Mule (1825)

WORSTED DRAFTING
Simple Suspended Spindle
Saxony Wheel
(Invented about 1555, but not introduced in England until eighteenth century)
Arkwright's Water Frame
(Patented 1769)

Used spindle-drafting for WOOLLEN yarns (about 1812–1830)

Used roller-drafting for WORSTED yarns.

Modern WOOLLEN Ring Spinning Frames
(Special form of drafting: for explanation of WOOLLEN drafting devices, see Chapter 10)

Modern WORSTED Spinning Frames
(Using the principle of roller drafting)

Modern WOOLLEN Mule

WORSTED Mule
(No longer produced)

---

*The expression 'on tenterhooks' owes its derivation to the hooks which held the cloth on the tenter frame.

†Messrs Wm Whiteley & Sons of Huddersfield produced their first tentering machine in 1854.

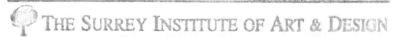

On market days the cloth was taken to the local market (sometimes in the unbleached and undyed state) to be sold to merchants, and more wool could then be bought for making other pieces of cloth.

This method of cloth manufacture naturally produced only a limited output, and as time went by some families of clothworkers, especially in the West Country and in the Eastern Countries, ceased to be their own masters. Instead they were employed on what today would be called commission work, by merchants who bought raw wool from the farmers and then put it out to different families to process. For example, one family would probably clean the wool and comb it, another would do the carding and spinning, another the weaving, each working in its own home, and the merchant paid them for the work they did for him. Merchants usually undertook the cloth finishing operations themselves with the aid of journeymen, or put the cloth out again to special groups of master fullers, bleachers and dyers. They then sold the finished cloth in the market.

Sometimes the merchant himself took over the spinning and weaving machinery and employed people to work it for him. Thus there developed the *clothiers* as these merchants came to be known.

In this way the domestic system was scattered all over the country, settling in hamlets and villages along the banks of streams which could supply water for processing. From some of these villages grew the textile towns of today (*see* Chapter 3).

WOOLLENS AND THE INDUSTRIAL REVOLUTION

The invention of machinery for making yarns and fabrics resulted in great changes in the textile industry of this country in the early nineteenth century. Many of the new machines were too large and expensive to be put in cottages. A new source of power had become available with the invention of the steam engine by James Watt in 1782. Thus factories or mills were built near the coalfields of Yorkshire and Lancashire to accommodate the new carding, spinning and weaving machines*, and this marked the end of the domestic system and the start of the factory era, a phase in history which is commonly known as the Industrial Revolution.

At first these developments aroused hostility in the minds of the handworkers. They feared unemployment and consequently riots followed in which gangs called Luddites wrecked workshops and destroyed textile machines. But this did

---

*Weaving became a factory process well after spinning, and even in 1812 most weaving was still done on the hand loom. Factory methods were applied in the woollen industry much later than in the worsted and cotton industries.

not deter the machine builders nor did it prevent more machinery from being installed in the factories, followed by still further inventions in the textile field. The fears of unemployment were groundless, for by the middle of the nineteenth century the new factories were absorbing more and more labour, markets were increasing and Britain was leading the way as the greatest textile manufacturing country in the world. From the time of the mid-nineteenth century the skills associated with woollen fabric production spread to the other industrialised areas of the world. This expansion in the location of the industry continues at the present time in the so-called 'developing regions' of the world although this, coupled with a marked increase in rates of productivity, has now resulted in a decline in the strength of the industry in some of the more traditional textile areas of the world.

The organisation within the industry does not differ greatly throughout the world but some of the woollen and worsted manufacturers specialized in definite types of cloth, and in certain districts different kinds of cloth gained their special prominence which remains to this day, particularly in the UK, as will be explained in Chapter 3.

The Distribution and Localization of the Woollen Industry

UNITED KINGDOM

Traditionally West Yorkshire (the old 'West Riding'), with adjoining parts of Lancashire forms the chief centre of the British wool textile industry and has a world-wide reputation for the manufacture of woollen and worsted cloths. An analysis of the information given in the latest (1975) Skinner's British Textile Directory suggests that, although the last decade has seen considerable change, this remains substantially true. In fact a very large proportion of Britain's worsteds and more than two-thirds of the woollens are manufactured there. The remainder of the woollens are chiefly supplied by the mills of the Scottish borders centred around Galashiels, Selkirk and Hawick. Some woollens are also produced in the West of England. The Hebrides are famous for their Harris tweeds, which are of course woollens, and there are also several mills in Wales, on the whole small ones, producing distinctive woollen fabrics, but they comprise almost a 'domestic' industry (Chapter 2).

THE WEST YORKSHIRE WOOL TEXTILE INDUSTRY

Woollen and worsted cloth manufacturing is not confined to any one district in West Yorkshire, although in some places one or the other is prominent. For example, Bradford has long been recognized as the centre of the country's worsted industry, and Huddersfield is famous for its woollens and also for weaving fine worsteds. Batley and Morley are well known for the manufacture of low woollens, and Dewsbury makes blankets in adddition to a variety of woollen cloths. The Colne and Holme valleys in the Huddersfield region specialize in making woollens of all types, whilst along the Calder valley, the production of blankets and other woollens predominates. Leeds is noted for the making-up of clothing, and some of the country's most important multiple tailors have factories in or around the city; there are also several woollen and worsted manufacturing firms in the district.

What are the dominant features which have contributed to the establishment of the industry in West Yorkshire? A simple answer cannot be given to this question for there a number of factors which have had their effects as far as the *woollen* side of the textile industry is concerned.

1. Before the Industrial Revolution the inhabitants of these districts were handworkers in carding, combing, spinning, weaving, dyeing and cloth finishing (Chapter 2). These processes were made mechanical chiefly in the late eighteenth and early nineteenth centuries; the introduction of the fly-shuttle in 1733 had created a demand for greater supplies of yarn; and spinning inventions followed to satisfy this demand. As time went by spinning became a *factory* process and this was followed later by weaving, but the changes in methods of production wrought by the inventors did not remove the industry from its location.

2. Traditional skill is an important element in wool manipulation and the industry cannot be considered apart from its workers, and vice versa. Thus both industry and workers became firmly established in the area.

3. The streams flowing down the valleys from the hills of the Pennines provided water power when the processes were first mechanized, and the settlement of the workers in the area was further stabilized during the steam era due to the proximity of the neighbourhood to the coal-fields.

4. Naturally as the mechanization of woollen and worsted processing gained impetus during the latter part of the eighteenth and in the early nineteeth centuries, other associated industries such as machine-making firms sprang up in and near the West Riding to cope with the demand for textile machinery. Some of these firms are still in existence today and together with others established later, have contributed in large measure to the importance of the UK woollen industry.

WOOLLENS IN SCOTLAND

Scotland is famous for its tweeds, Cheviots* and Saxonies*, and also for its knitwear. Galashiels, Hawick, Selkirk, Peebles, and adjacent districts feature amongst the important centres of the Scotch Tweed industry, and there are also woollen mills around Aberdeen, Elgin, Inverness and still further north and east, but some of them are only small. Cashmere and lambs' wool are also spun in these areas. The Glasgow district has several textile firms, whilst the spinning mills of Kilmarnock are engaged chiefly on the production of woollen-spun yarns for the carpet industry, dealt with elsewhere.

Harris tweeds are made in the islands of the Hebrides.

THE WEST OF ENGLAND WOOLLEN TRADE

This was formerly a very important textile area, but the number of firms has declined in recent years.

*See Chapter 14.

The industry is situated in several different districts rather widely separated. For example, the textile area of the West Country extends roughly from Witney in Oxfordshire (famous for its blankets) as far as Totnes in Devon, and it also includes such places as Trowbridge, Westbury, Stroud, Chipping Norton, Wellington (in Somerset), and several other towns, although today there are less than a dozen firms in all. Nevertheless, some of the finest high-class woollens are made there, especially cloths which have been milled and raised (*see* Chapter 14), such as flannels, billiard cloths, blankets, meltons, beavers and tennis-ball covers. In addition to woollens, many of the firms in the West of England also weave and finish good quality worsteds made from yarns spun elsewhere.

LANCASHIRE

Those parts of Lancashire adjoining the borders of West Yorkshire produce woollens similar to the cloths of Huddersfield and district; at one time the Rochdale area was specially noted for its flannels. The Rossendale valley is famous for its felt-making; some of the cloths are *pressed* felts and others are woven from yarns produced on the woollen system and finished by woollen-finishing techniques (*see* Chapter 14). Many of these fabrics find applications in industry, for example in printing and paper making. Felts are also produced in other parts of Lancashire and in a few other places in the UK.

OTHER WOOLLEN MANUFACTURING DISTRICTS IN THE UK

With one or two exceptions the *Welsh* woollen mills are very small units mainly producing flannel shirtings, blankets, travel rugs, honeycomb quilts and tweeds. As regards woollen manufacturing in *Ireland,* tweeds and blankets are made in the Cork and Donegal districts of Eire, whilst the woollen industry of Northern Ireland is only on a small scale.

Now that the widespread use of electricity has rendered the woollen industry no longer dependent on the proximity to the coal-fields for its source of power, and because transport is much easier than in former days, there appears to be no real need for the industry to be tied to one particular district. A few firms have established branch factories or even moved entirely to areas of more abundant labour, but in the main the UK woollen and worsted industries continue to remain concentrated in the places where the mills were first established during the Industrial Revolution.

EUROPE

Most European countries have a well developed textile industry, included in which is the manufacture of woollen and worsted fabrics. As in the case of the

UK, the range of raw materials used includes re-manufactured fibres, necessitating rag and waste processing facilities. Of particular importance are France, Germany and Belgium. Much of the main textile industry of these countries are located in the Lille, Aachen and Verviers regions.

Italy is also of particular importance in terms of the production of woollen fabrics. Both the Scandinavian countries and those of the Iberian peninsula produce fabrics for home and export. Little information is currently available regarding the statistics of fabric production in East European countries; however, as indicated in Chapter 5, Russia is an important wool producing country, much of the wool grown there being primarily suited for woollen-type processing.

THE AMERICAS

Almost all the countries of both North and South America have active textile industries producing woollen-type fabrics. The largest industry is probably that of the USA. This industry originated in the New England States, particularly in Massachusetts. However the textile industry of this area is now much declined, becoming much more widely located, particularly in the states of North Carolina and Pennsylvania.

The South American countries also produce woollen fabrics, many of them having an industry which includes rag processing, spinning and manufacturing.

ASIA

The textile industry is traditionally one of the earliest industries established in what are now described as 'developing countries'. However it must be remembered that many of these areas have had long established domestic industries. India, Pakistan and Hong Kong produce woollen fabrics, as do most of the Middle Eastern countries. Many of these are now well established, for example the first textile factory in Iran (Persia) was opened almost 50 years ago.

AUSTRALASIA

Both New Zealand and Australia use their home produced wools for conversion into woollen and worsted fabrics. Additionally, because they have other large textile industries they will reprocess remanufactured materials. The end-products are used both for internal and export purposes.

NOTE:

It should be noted that although they use woollen yarns amongst various others, carpets and knitting are industries in themselves, so they will not be dealt with in this book. The reader is referred to other works for further information.

CHAPTER 4

The Organization of the Woollen Industry

In general it can be said that the worsted industry is *horizontally* organized, whereas the woollen industry is *vertically* organized. Briefly stated, this means that several distinct firms are usually involved in the conversion of raw wool to saleable worsted fabric whereas in the woollen trade it is quite common to find one mill taking in the raw material, processing it, and delivering the finished fabric to the cloth merchant or to the maker-up.

It will be appreciated that for either the woollen or the worsted industry to operate successfully and economically it is preferable for all those firms that participate in the manufacture of a woollen or a worsted fabric to be concentrated in or around a particular area, and this frequently happens as has been explained in previous chapters.

The division of the *worsted* trade into distinct sections is partly due to the large number of processes involved between the fleece and the fabric, and also to the piecemeal invention of worsted machinery for the various sections of the industry, viz. weaving, spinning and combing. The *woollen* trade, on the other hand, has fewer sections of processing between raw material and finished fabric. Briefly the work of a woollen manufacturer consists of blending, carding, spinning, weaving, dyeing and finishing, with some ancillary processes. As will be seen in a later chapter it is almost essential for the blending, carding and spinning to be done in one mill, and because there needs to be very close liaison between the blending, designing and finishing departments owing to the vast variety of raw materials and cloths encountered in woollen manufacture, it is convenient if these departments can be together also. It is possible for a woollen cloth to be produced—from raw material to finished fabric—in a much smaller manufacturing unit than would be required for a worsted cloth, so it is a more practical proposition for all the processes involved in the manufacture of woollens to be done in one mill. However, there are also firms which specialize in the separate sections of woollen manufacture, namely yarn production, weaving, dyeing and finishing, as explained later in this chapter.

This state of affairs is not confined to West Yorkshire; it occurs in the other woollen and worsted manufacturing areas of the world.

THE MARKETING OF RAW MATERIALS FOR THE WOOLLEN INDUSTRY
The woollen industry uses a very extensive range of raw materials in the
manufacture of the many types of woven apparel fabrics, knitwear, blankets,
carpets and furnishing fabrics. In addition to many different types of virgin wool,
each suitable for a specific purpose, the woollen trade uses large quantities of
waste fibres from the worsted mills and also shoddy and mungo produced from
both new and old rags and clippings. The marketing of raw materials used in
woollen manufacture will therefore be dealt with briefly under three headings—
    1. Raw wool,
    2. Re-manufactured materials, and
    3. Man-made staple fibres.

Raw wool
The three means of disposal of a wool clip by the wool grower are—
(i)   Local auctions,
(ii)   Private sales,
(iii)   Direct shipment (in the case of overseas growers) for sale at the Bradford
auctions or elsewhere.

A large proportion of Australian, New Zealand and South African wool is
sold by public auction in the country of origin and then shipped to the buyers
in the consuming countries.

In South America, both Argentina and Uruguay market wool by private
treaty. The same system applies to the United States, but most of the wool
grown there is for home consumption.

As an alternative to local auctions, the overseas wool grower can send his
wool to the auction sales at Bradford Auction of Overseas Wools.

Being near to all the major manufacturing centres, Bradford is a good 'spot'
market from which supplies can be personally selected for delivery at short
notice. All the shorn wool production of the UK is marketed through the
British Wool Marketing Board, set up in 1950, an explanation of which is given
in books on British wools.

The financial arrangements involved in wool purchasing (including futures
marketing) are beyond the scope of this book, and the reader is directed
elsewhere for details (*see* Bibliography).

The types of wool supplied by the various wool-growing countries are
discussed in Chapter 5.

Only the larger woollen manufacturers have buyers or representatives at the
wool auctions. Others prefer to buy wool from wool merchants who specialize
in appraising and buying at the sales. These firms buy raw wool in reasonably
large quantities either at home or abroad, and sell batches of wool to spinners
and manufacturers (and also to 'top makers' in the worsted industry). In and

around Bradford there will be found numerous firms of this type. Some merely operate from an office, whereas others have large warehouses and may employ wool sorters (*see* Chapter 6). In addition many wool merchants add to their trade by dealing in noils, a by-product of the worsted combing process, and also in waste from various textile processes (which can be treated and re-used); there are also other firms who specialize in these commodities.

Re-manufactured Materials

Old rags are collected by the *tatter* or rag-and-bone man who usually sells them to the marine store, where a rough sorting may take place before the rags are sent either to be auctioned or sold to the rag merchant. On the other hand, *new* rags are clippings left over by the maker-up or tailor (today chiefly multiple tailoring factories) when garments are made, and these are also auctioned or sold to the rag merchant.

All rags, whether old or new, are sorted into types, qualities and shades by the rag merchant's employees, and sold to the shoddy manufacturer who transforms them into a fibrous state called either shoddy or mungo; the difference is explained on page 2 and in Chapter 7. Some firms deal in both rags and shoddies.

Other merchants sell wastes which they have bought from worsted mills and sorted into larger lots. Such materials include noils (*see* page 2), laps, roving waste, hard or thread waste, and brush waste, all of which can be used for making into various types of cloth on the *woollen* system, but are unsuitable or too short in fibre length for *worsted* processing.

Man-made Staple Fibres

These are purchased either direct from the man-made fibre producers (e.g. Courtaulds, Monsanto, ICI, etc) or through an agent. They are discussed in Chapter 5.

WOOLLEN PROCESSES

In addition to those concerns which carry out *all* the processes of woollen manufacture under one roof—from blending to cloth finishing—there are also firms which carry out one or two processes only. For example there are *woollen spinners* (often referred to as *yarn spinners*) who buy raw materials, blend, card, spin and sometimes twist or *fold* the yarns and then sell them either to cloth manufacturers to knitting firms or to carpet mills.

Again, there are similar spinning firms that do some or all of these processes on commission; this means that the woollen manufacturer (usually when the weights on his order book exceed his own productive capacity) send his raw materials or a ready-prepared blend of his raw materials to the *commission spinner* to be made, at a charge, into yarn for him, and at all times the material remains the property of the woollen manufacturer. There are advantages and disadvantages in this arrangement both to the woollen manufacturer and to the commission firm. In busy periods a completely self-contained vertical firm of woollen manufacturers is more fortunately placed than those of its competitors who usually or always rely on having certain processes done for them on commission, in that it does not have to take its turn at these commission firms. On the other hand, in slack times, vertical firms may have plant and operatives idle. There are disadvantages too for the commission firms, for they are busy when the rest of the industry is busy, but when there is a recession in trade, they may have difficulty in finding sufficient orders to keep their plant running and their operatives fully occupied.

Just as there are separate firms of woollen spinners, both for sales yarns and on commission work, so there are firms of woollen manufacturers, some of whom buy their yarn from the spinners, process it and sell the finished cloth, some who buy yarn and have it processed into cloth for them on a commission basis, and others who actually do the commission weaving to a specified design, cloth-weight and dimensions as explained in Chapter 13.

Some woollen manufacturers have their own cloth finishing and dyeing departments, although it is quite common for them to have dyeing and finishing 'done out' by what are sometimes called *country finishers.*

TECHNICAL EDUCATION, WORK STUDY AND RESEARCH
The UK woollen and worsted industries are well supplied with facilities for technical education in the universities, polytechnics and technical colleges. The Wool, Jute and Flax Industry Training Board was established in 1964 to aid training, technical education and recruitment, although the Wool (and Allied) Textile Employers' Council had its own Recruitment Education and Training Department and also a Work Study Centre for many years before that.

Research and technical services are provided by Wira* from its laboratories at Leeds and Galashiels. In addition the universities and polytechnics also do research, as do many of the large industrial organizations. Most wool textile firms now have their own quality control departments.

SEQUENCE OF WOOLLEN PROCESSES
Before explaining in detail the individual processes of the woollen industry, it will be useful to list then in the order used and to outline briefly the function of each.

*Formerly called the Wool Industries Research Association. Established in 1918, Wira was for many years familiarly known as 'Torridon', the name of the original premises in Headingley.

NAME OF PROCESS OR OPERATION	FUNCTION OF THE PROCESS
For Virgin Wool	
1. (a) Wool sorting	Dividing the fleece manually into various qualities.
(b) Wool scouring	Removal of wool fat, sweat and other impurities from raw wool, usually by means of heated water, soap and soda-ash or other detergents.
(c) Carbonizing (if necessary)	Removal of cellulosic impurity (e.g. burrs) by acid treatment followed by neutralization by alkali.
(d) Wool drying	Removal of excess water left in the wool.
For Rags, etc	
1. (a) Rag sorting	Allocating the rags to various categories according to colour, type, quality and whether new or old.
(b) Rag pulling	The operation of reducing new or old rags to a fibrous state, preceded if necessary by shaking, dusting and rag-carbonizing and/or dyeing.
(c) Garnetting	Reducing thread wastes to a fibrous form in a special machine containing cylinders and rollers covered with saw-like metallic teeth.
For all Fibres	
2. Blending	The mixing together (in suitable machinery) of different fibrous materials for price, colour, quality, regularity and/or effect purposes.
3. Carding (a collective term including scribbling, carding and condensing)	Disentanglement and intimate mixing together of the fibres and colours, removal mechanically of vegetable matter and any hard threads present, and delivery of the material in a number of twistless slubbings.
4. Spinning Alternative machines— (a) Mule (b) Ring-frame	The formation from the slubbings of a yarn of the required thickness (i.e. weight per unit length) and number of turns of twist per unit length.

NAME OF PROCESS OR OPERATION	FUNCTION OF THE PROCESS
5. Twisting (if required) (sometimes termed 'folding')	Combining together two or more spun yarns, with the addition of twist for the purpose of providing strength, regularity, surface characteristics, special effects or a combination of colours.
6. Yarn preparation— (a) Reeling	Forming the yarns into hanks of a definite length, for dyeing or for hand-knitting or carpet yarns.
(b) Winding	Transferring single or twisted yarns on to cones, cheeses or pirns for weaving or knitting purposes.
(c) Warping	Placing single or folded yarns in a predetermined order, side by side on a beam for use in weaving.
7. Preparatory to weaving (including dressing, twisting-in or tying-in, looming)	Drawing the warp threads from the warp-beam through the healds and reed of the loom in predetermined order according to the design required in the fabric.
8. Weaving	A mechanical process performed on a loom whereby warp and weft yarns are interlaced in correct manner according to the required design in order to form a cloth.
9. Perching	Inspection of the woven fabric and marking of any faults detected.
10. Burling and mending	The removal of minor defects or extraneous substances by manual labour.
11. Cloth finishing	Treatment of the fabric by both wet and dry processes to produce the required effect and handle.

N.B. The dyeing process may be applied at one of the following stages—
    (i)   After wool scouring (loose wool dyeing),
    (ii)   Before rag pulling (rag dyeing),
    (iii)   After 6(a) or 6(b) (yarn dyeing),
    (iv)   During 11 (piece dyeing).
These are explained in Chapter 15.

CHAPTER 5

Raw materials for the Woollen Industry

It was mentioned in Chapter 1 that in addition to pure wool, a wide variety of other fibrous materials is available to the woollen industry. In the present chapter wool, re-manufactured materials, man-made fibres and some other fibres that are used in blends will be dealt with briefly*.

WOOL

Wool has been said to represent nearly two per cent of the total value of international trade and to rank sixth in the list of primary commodities. Sheep of some kind are reared in nearly every country in the world. Although sheep numbers have shown a small decline in recent years World Wool Statistics show that at present the total number of sheep in the world is estimated as approximately 900 millions, producing 2434 million kilograms of greasy wool in 1973-4 equivalent to 1404 million kilograms clean, of which about four-fifths is suitable for manufacture into clothing.

Not all of this wool however goes into the *woollen* trade. As previously noted the worsted industry uses only pure virgin wool; care must be exercised in the choice of wool for worsteds and usually twelve months' growth is required. The woollen trade can, however, use shorter wools. In some countries sheep are shorn at shorter intervals than a year, and there are also on the market wools removed from the skins of slaughtered sheep. The fibre length of the latter class of wool naturally depends on the time that has elapsed between the last shearing and the slaughtering, which could take place at any time of the year.

The length of fibre partly determines whether a particular wool is suitable for processing on the worsted system or whether it is more suitable for the woollen trade (Chapter 1).

TYPES OF WOOL†

The various breeds of sheep throughout the world can be grouped under four main headings according to the use that is made of them, i.e:

*Detailed information will be found in books listed in the Bibliography.

†Various hairs are also used in the woollen industry, but space does not permit an account of these, e.g. mohair, alpaca, cashmere, camel, angora, vicuna.

      1. For wool,

      2. For mutton,

      3. Dual-purpose, and

      4. Multi-purpose, which includes producing hides and manure and supplying milk and cheese (as in some Central European and Asiatic countries with nomadic tribes).

The types available to the trade may be broadly classified into:

      1. Merino or botany,

      2. Crossbreds—fine, medium and coarse, and

      3. Carpet wool types;

but there are many grades of wool within these groups (*see* later in this Chapter regarding British wools). Generally speaking, merino wool fibres have the finest diameter and shortest length, whilst carpet wools are long fibred with coarse diameters and crossbreds occupy an intermediate position.

WOOL-GROWING COUNTRIES OF IMPORTANCE TO THE UK WOOL TRADE

The greatest weights of wool of interest to the UK are produced by Australia, New Zealand, South Africa and South America. The carpet industry is also interested in East Indian wools.

    Australia produces large quantities of botany and crossbred wools for both the woollen and worsted industries. In fact more wool is grown in Australia than anywhere else in the world, amounting to almost a third of the world's total clip. About three-quarters of the sheep are merinos, found chiefly in New South Wales, South Queensland, south-west Victoria, the south-west of Western Australia and the south-east of South Australia.

    New Zealand sheep are mainly crossbreds, reared for mutton as well as wool. Nevertheless they provide a large and regular supply of medium and fine crossbred wools. Approximately ninety-seven per cent of New Zealand's total clip is classed as crossbred apparel wool; on the whole the climate is too damp for merinos, and the west coast is too wet and mountainous for sheep, so they are found on the drier eastern side. New Zealand ranks third after Australia and the Soviet Union amongst the world's wool producers, and takes second place to Australia as an exporter of wool. New Zealand is the world's largest producer and exporter of crossbred apparel wool.

    South Africa is a dry country and so favours merino sheep production. It is now the world's second largest grower of merino wool, and also supplies some carpet wools. Most of the sheep are found around Cape Province, the Orange Free State, Natal and the Transvaal. At one time, owing to the practice of shearing when it happened to be convenient or most profitable, often at intervals of less than a year, many South African wools were too short for the Bradford worsted trade, but they were very useful for woollen processing.

South America is a large wool producer. Argentina supplies the greatest quantity, which consists of merinos, crossbreds and some native carpet wools. Uruguay comes second with merinos and fine crossbreds. In both countries crossbred wools predominate, and a large number of the sheep are dual-purpose animals, being kept primarily for mutton and secondarily for wool, this accounting for the low percentage of merino wool that is exported.

The United States of America and Canada produce large quantities of merino and crossbred wools but these are used chiefly in the home industries of those countries.

British sheep are producers of:

1. Long or lustre wools,
2. Down or short wools, and
3. Mountain or coarse wools.

The climate is too damp for merinos. Although they produce a great deal of wool for the woollen and worsted industries, sheep are also kept to a large extent for meat and manure, whilst some of the best sheep are sold abroad for crossbreeding purposes.

Other countries. Russia pastures millions of sheep which produce various qualities of wool for home consumption, but few of its wools are comparable with the growths of the British Commonwealth and other leading wool producing countries.

Some merinos are grown in Spain, Germany and Austria, whilst France and the Scandinavian countries have sheep which produce wool mainly of a crossbred character, most of which is used locally.

Asiatic wools are usually coarse and often of various colours; these find uses mainly in the woollen industry.

RE-MANUFACTURED MATERIALS

In general these comprise shoddy, mungo, extract, noils, flocks and various textile processing wastes. The terms *shoddy* and *mungo* have been defined and explained in Chapter 1. Both are produced from rags as described in Chapter 7. Rags can be divided into many classifications, but a detailed account cannot be given here.

Extract is derived from cloths comprising cotton-and-wool; the cotton is removed *(extracted)* by carbonizing *(see* Chapter 7) and the wool which remains is pulled, as for shoddy and mungo.

Noils are pure wool of short fibre length, separated from the longer wool fibres during worsted combing. The long fibres are put into parallel formation to make what is known as a worsted *top.* Top slivers are sometimes purposely broken into shorter lengths to produce *broken top* for use in the woollen trade.

Flocks are a by-product of such operations as milling and cropping in cloth finishing. They are very short in fibre length.

Wastes may be generally classified as soft and hard. Soft wastes consist of twistless materials such as worsted top sliver waste and some slubbings and rovings, and also slubbing waste from woollen carding. Hard wastes contain twist and include waste yarn from woollen and worsted spinning, twisting, winding, warping and weaving. They usually require garnetting (*see* Chapter 7).

MAN-MADE FIBRES

Man-made staple fibres* are being used in increasing quantities on existing plant in the UK woollen industry. They include fibres such as viscose rayon, triacetate, polyamide, polyester, acrylic, etc, produced by various UK and overseas firms. Man-made staple fibres can be blended with wool, shoddy and hairs, or sometimes be spun alone on the woollen system. The processing is usually very similar to that for wool, provided that comparable fibre lengths and diameters are used. For example, when blending 'Fibro' with 64s quality wool, 3.3 decitex 64mm staple fibre is recommended. Certain modifications to existing processing conditions are sometimes necessary, but the suppliers of the particular staple fibre will readily advise on the optimum speeds and settings. This book is mainly concerned with processing *wool* on the woollen system, and for further information on the use of man-made fibres the reader is advised to consult the producer of the particular fibre.

OTHER FIBRES

Sometimes fibres such as cotton, or real silk in waste-form, are used in woollen blends. For example, 'Angola' yarn is made from a blend of wool and cotton, spun on the woollen system. A small percentage of cotton may be used in a low woollen blend to give strength to the yarn, although nylon is used for this purpose in those blends for which the price can be afforded.

Some cheaper blazer cloths have cotton warps and woollen wefts, whilst fabrics are also made with worsted or 'Fibro't warps and woollen wefts.

WOOL TRADE STATISTICS

For up-to-date information on the weights of the different textile fibres used in the various sections of the wool textile industry, the reader is directed to current volumes of the directories listed in the Bibliography. These directories are available in public libraries. They also contain other useful statistical data on the wool textile industry.

*Man-made staple fibre is made by cutting or breaking continuous filament into lengths suitable for the spinning system in question (e.g. woollen, worsted, cotton, etc.)

†A trade name for viscose staple.

CHAPTER 6

Wool Sorting, Scouring, Drying and Carbonizing

Raw wool is contaminated with impurities which are usually allowed to remain in the wool until after it is sold and in the country of yarn or cloth manufacture. The percentage of these impurities varies very considerably in different classes of wool; for example, a merino (or botany) may contain 45—55 per cent impurity, whereas some English wools only show a loss of 20—25 per cent after the cleansing processes.

These impurities fall into three main classes, each with several subdivisions. Table 2 gives details, together with an indication of the means of removal.

TABLE 2
Impurities Present on Raw Wool

Class of impurity	Type of impurity		Remarks	Means of removal
Natural	Secretions:	Sweat ('suint'); grease or fat	Always present	Scouring
	Accretions:	Kemps and black fibres	Breed characteristics	Sorting
	Excretions:	Dung and urine		Sorting and scouring
Acquired	Animal: Bugs, ticks, lice			Carding
	Vegetable: Burrs, dry grass		Picked up by the sheep during grazing	Carding and sometimes carbonising
	Mineral: Earth, sand, dirt		do.	Shaking and scouring
Applied	(i)	Tar and paint	For identification	Sorting
	(ii)	Branding fluids	For identification	Sorting and/or scouring
	(iii)	Sheep-dips and -salves	For antiseptic purposes	Scouring

WOOL SORTING

The fibres in a fleece of wool vary in length, diameter and general condition from one part of the sheep to another*. In order to 'get the best out' of a lot of wool, it must be sorted. This is a highly skilled manual process whereby each fleece is divided up into various *qualities,* and it involves sight and touch. Both these senses have to be highly trained to sort wool to the satisfaction of the passer, who knows exactly what is required from each lot. The work is conducted in a good light, preferably facing north, by men who have served a proper apprenticeship to this highly skilled job.

The sorter divides the fleece into various *matchings,* the real difference between which is the average fibre fineness or diameter. He looks for length, waviness and character of tip, and feels the wool for handle, density, strength and soundness. In addition to sorting the sound wool into various categories, he rejects material heavily contaminated with impurity as shown in Table 2. The wool sorters' matchings are given special names or quality numbers such as 70s, 64s, 58s etc; the higher the number the better the quality of the wool. The main trade classifications and their average quality numbers are:

1. Merino wools — 60s and upwards (approx. fibre diameter 25μ and finer)
2. Fine crossbreds — 56s—58s (approx. 28μ—25μ)
3. Medium crossbreds — 46s—50s (approx 33μ—31μ)
4. Low crossbreds — 44s and below (approx. 34μ and coarser)

The derivation of these numbers is explained in textbooks specifically relating to wool. Many firms have their own distinguishing terms.

It is probably not realized that the wool sorter was one of the pioneers of *quality control* in the wool trade!

WOOL SCOURING

Wool is usually scoured before being processed into yarn so as to remove grease, sweat and mineral impurity. Scouring is sometimes omitted for certain lower-grade qualities intended for the carpet or blanket trade and these are carded (*see* Chapter 9) in the greasy state. The grease left in may assist as a fibre lubricant in processing but the dirt which is also present can be objectionable. In any case the grease must be removed later, so the present-day tendency is to scour such greasy wools before the blending and carding processes, and then apply a carding oil in blending for the purpose of fibre lubrication, since this results in cleaner machinery and working conditions, as well as the elimination of possible faults in dyeing and finishing.

---

* Wool fleeces are separated into different classes (each class as homogeneous as possible) before baling and selling. This is called classing and assists buyers to obtain their requirements. This is an important activity of the British Wool Marketing Board.

Raw wool is scoured in large machines, specially constructed for mass production. The process may be carried out in two different ways:

1. Emulsion scouring, and
2. The solvent system.

The first mentioned is by far the most popular, so will be the only one discussed in this book.

EMULSION SCOURING

The cleansing of wool by the emulsion system is usually performed in sets of scouring *bowls* (sometimes known as a washing set); this may be preceded by a shaking machine and/or a water steeping process to remove, as far as possible, the heavy sand and water-soluble impurities before the scouring process proper.

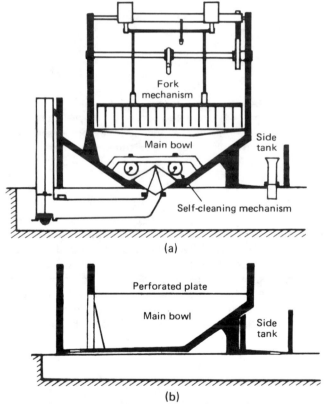

(a)

(b)

FIG.2 Transverse sections of 180-cm (6-ft) wide wool-scouring bowls with side settling tanks.

(a) Self-cleaning bowl   (b) Non-self-cleaning bowl
(Petrie & McNaught Ltd)

he washing set consists of a series of tanks or bowls, usually three to five in umber according to the amount of impurity to be removed, separated from ach other by pairs of revolving squeeze rollers; the whole apparatus makes an utomatic unit for effective wool cleansing. Heated water, soap and alkali (or ther detergents) are the scouring agents used, assisted by agitation from the echanical arrangement which propels the wool through the bowls.

The wool is fed automatically into the first bowl of the series from a hopper a rate depending on the size of the bowl and the type of wool*. When it falls to the scouring liquor it is first thoroughly wetted out by some form of merser (*ducker* or *posser*) and is then moved slowly forward through the wl by a set of forks, helped by a flow of water in the same direction as shown in Plate 3. Each bowl may have a depth of about a metre (one yard), but, as shown in Fig.2, about 40cm (15 inches) from the top of the bowl there is a perforated metal sheet which acts as a false bottom and prevents the wool from sinking to the bottom of the main bowl and possibly getting out of control, but at the same time allows a large volume of water to be used, thus obviating frequent changes.

Heavily-weighted squeeze rollers at the delivery end of each bowl take out the dirty water which passes into a side settling-tank, where a partial separation of grease and dirt takes place, the liquor being pumped back into the main bowl. The wool emerging from the squeeze rollers passes into the next bowl for further treatment. The conditions maintained in a wool scouring set vary from firm to firm and often within a firm. Table 3 gives some details of a set in use for scouring greasy merino wool. Wools which give higher yields, such as greasy crossbreds or English wools, will be processed at a higher rate of production, and probably a three-bowl set will suffice, but with a different form of propulsion mechanism consisting of rakes, which provide more agitation than the forks used for merinos.

Removal of Impurity from the Wash Bowl

A large amount of impurity is removed from the wool and left behind in the bowls. The major portion of this impurity is left in the first bowl, and means have been devised for getting rid of it from the bowl as soon as it reaches the bowl bottom. As shown in the transverse section of a scouring bowl in Fig.2(a) special mechanisms can be incorporated in the first bowl. These consist of spiral-bladed shafts along and within the specially-shaped bowl bottom. One-half of the length of the shafts has a right-hand screw and the other half a left-hand screw. The shafts rotate slowly and their blades scrape up the impurity and direct it to a central position where the bowl outlet is sited. A timing mechanism controls the opening and closing of the valve to let out the

*Up to 1500kg (3,300 lb) per hour is claimed by Petrie & McNaught Ltd for their 180-cm (6 ft) wide bowl, but for merino wools in practice the production would be lower than this e.g. 910kg (2,000 lb) per hour of greasy wool.

TABLE 3
Suggested procedure for scouring merino wools—average yield 50 per cent[1]

	Bowls			
	1st	2nd	3rd	4th
Length (metres)	9.14	7.3	6.39	5.48
Length (ft)	30	24	21	18
Capacity (litres)	8,183	6,819	5,682	4,546
Capacity (gallons)	1,800	1,500	1,250	1,000
Temperature ($^\circ$C)	54.4	51.6	48.9	46.1
Temperature ($^\circ$F)	130	125	120	115
Soap (approx per cent[2])	0.5	0.5	0.2	—
Alkali (approx per cent[2])	0.2	0.1	—	—
Time in bowl (minutes)	3	2½	2	1½

1. See text for further details of the machinery.
2. Percentages are based on the weight of liquor in the bowl (1 gallon = 10lb = 4.546 litres). Add one-fifth extra if self-cleaning bowls are used.

accumulated sludge. An elaborate system of pipes and float-valves is very effective in passing the liquor back from the second bowl to the first to make good the deficiency due to loss through the outlet valve. The second bowl is replenished from the third and so on and the final bowl receives additions of clean water.

When the wool is delivered from the last bowl it should be lofty and soft-handling with a 'clean' smell.

DETERGENTS AND EFFLUENT RECOVERY
Soap and soda ash (sodium carbonate) are effective scouring agents for wool scouring and have no deleterious effects on the wool fibre if properly applied. The last bowl of a washing set should be a warm water rinse to remove the remaining traces of impurity, soap and alkali. In the last quarter of a century, as for household washing, various synthetic detergents have been introduced as a substitute for soap, but the scouring technique usually requires some modification. Since some of the impurities removed by wool scouring can be worked up into valuable products such as various greases and lanoline for cosmetics and pharmaceutical uses, it is sometimes worthwhile to purify the spent scouring liquors as is done by various sewage works and some of the larger wool-combing mills in the worsted trade.

NEW DEVELOPMENTS
During the last ten years several modifications to the machinery used in emulsion scouring have been introduced by both UK and Continental machinery makers. These continue to use soap and alkali (or detergent) as the main scouring agents but in some cases quite substantial improvements in the

efficiency of the unit have been proved. One of the foremost of these is the Petrie/ Wira Improved Scouring Set (see Plate 4). The set continues to use the harrow system to move the wool through the bowls, but differs from a conventional plant in the following features:

1. Bowl lengths are shorter; the total length of the 4-bowl set is only 21m 590 (70ft 10in) compared with a normal 32m 308 (106ft).

2. Immersion times are similar to those in conventional processing because slower harrow speeds and a shorter stroke are used. The stream of wool in the bowl is correspondingly thicker and is therefore restrained from undue movement and hence entanglement.

3. The set can be run continuously without stoppage for scouring liquor change. Each bowl consists of a main tank and two side tanks (Plate 4) with a total capacity similar to a conventional set. After 8 hours running, one side tank is isolated, emptied, and recharged with fresh scouring solution. The circulating pump is then switched over to circulate the fresh liquor, and the other side tank is isolated and recharged.

4. Water usage is around 2.27 litres (½ gallon) per 0.5kg (1lb) of scoured wool, compared with the average conventional usage of twice this amount. A 120-cm (4-ft) wide set will produce approximately 680kg (1500lb) per hour of scoured merino wool.

WOOL DRYING

Despite the use of the heavily-weighted squeeze rollers at the final delivery of the wash bowls, the wool leaving a washing set contains about 50 per cent of moisture which must be removed before further processing. This can be effected either (i) *physically* by evaporation or (ii) *mechanically* by squeezing or by centrifugal force in a hydro-extractor (*see* Chapter 14). The latter method does not reduce the moisture content sufficiently for efficient subsequent processing, and also, being an intermittent process, it is time-consuming and costly in labour. Therefore, hot-air drying is usually practised after wool scouring.

In the more primitive days of woollen manufacture when wool was washed in rivers and streams, it was presumably dried by hand-wringing or by the action of the wind and sun in the open air. This method must have been haphazard and unreliable. Drying by hot air is popular today and is based on the fact that moisture can be transferred from the wet wool if brought in contact with heated air. The capacity of air to hold moisture is increased by a rise in temperature, as may be seen from the following figures taken from *The Wira Textile Data Book*. Saturated air at 10°C contains 9.4 grams of moisture per cubic metre; at 40°C the amount is 51 grams; at 70°C the amount is 197 grams; and at 90°C the amount held has risen to 419 grams.

This phenomenon is made use of in wool drying, but hot air in the presence of wet wool is not sufficient. Before it becomes saturated with moisture the air must be removed, or condensation of water may occur. Adequate pressure is necessary to force the air to do more than simply impinge on the surface of the wool staples

under treatment; it must be sufficient to ensure that the interior of the staples is
dried also. Five conditions therefore, are essential for efficient wool drying; they
may be summarized as:

1. A high but not *too* high temperature of air to ensure adequate moisture
removal without scorching the wool,

2. A sufficient volume of dry air for its moisture-absorbing capacity to be
utilized to the utmost,

3. Continuous movement and openness of the wool,

4. Movement of the air throughout the wool,

5. Removal of the air when it becomes saturated (so as to prevent re-deposition
or condensation of moisture) and its replacement by further dry warm air.

These factors have been taken into consideration by machinery makers when
designing modern wool dryers. The wool is delivered from the last squeeze of the
scouring set into the feed hopper of the dryer, and requires no handling at this
point since the drying machine is constructed to deal adequately with the
output of the wash bowls.

WOOL-DRYING MACHINES

The development of the wool-dryer during the past century has resulted in a
continuous improvement in efficiency in terms of economy of steam and power
consumption, together with the minimum use of floor space. The present stage
in this development is the use of hot air at about $82°C$ ($180°F$) which can be
made to flow with or against the wool, but at all times over-drying must be
avoided. A modern single-passage dryer is shown in Fig. 3. In this machine an
automatic feed attached to the last scouring bowl of the washing set drops the
wool on to a single perforated steel brattice revolving the full length of the
several chambers. The drying arrangements consist of several compartments
through which hot air at varying controllable temperatures passes alternately in
an upward and downward direction through the wool resting on the brattice;
fans are suitably positioned in relation to the steam-heating pipes to effect the
alternation of draught. This method of air circulation helps to keep the wool in
an open condition, suitable for later processes. The temperature of the air
passing into each chamber may be regulated and it is usual for unheated
atmospheric air to be used in the last compartment of the dryer. Ready access to
every part of the machine is facilitated by the use of sliding doors.

A more recent type of drying machine is shown in Fig. 4. Different versions
are now made by several firms* and consist essentially of a chamber containing
in sequence two, three or four large revolving perforated drums each about four
feet in diameter and three feet or more wide. Heated air is sucked from the
chamber through the perforations into the interior of the drums. By a carefully
planned arrangement of fans and baffles inside the drums, together with heaters,

---

*E.g. Fleissner Ltd and Petrie & McNaught Ltd.

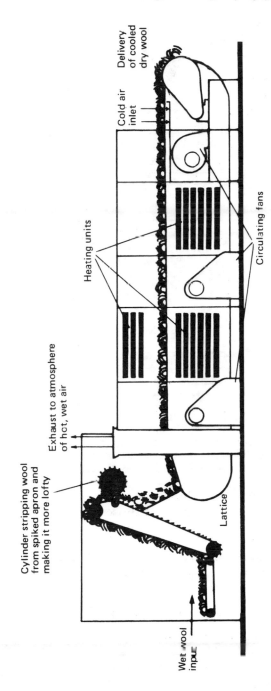

FIG.3 Single-passage wool drying machine
(Petrie & McNaught Ltd)

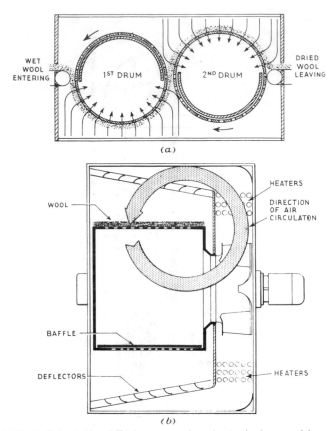

FIG. 4 *Principles of Fleissner suction-drum drying machine.*
(a) Side elevation   (b) Cross-section of second drum
(Fleissner Ltd, Bradford)

deflector plates and baffles in the chamber, the wet wool is held by suction
first against the lower half of the perforated surface of one drum and is then
transferred to the upper half of the second drum, and so on; hot air is drawn
through it into the drums, taking with it the moisture absorbed from the wool.
This air can be recirculated for further use or passed through an exhaust duct.
Drum dryers are economical in power, steam consumption, labour and floor
space (*see also* Chapter 15).

WOOL CARBONIZING

Vegetable matter, such as burrs, seeds and straw can be removed from wool
either:
1. *Mechanically*—just before and/or during carding, or
2. *Chemically*—immediately after wool scouring or during cloth finishing.

The stage chosen depends on the type and quantity, the method of processing and the resultant fabric. The worsted industry usually prefers mechanical burr removal, whilst in woollen manufacture both mechanical and chemical means are in use. Mechanical methods are described in Chapter 9.

The chemical methods depend on the fact that vegetable matter is cellulosic and can be converted into a black brittle hydrocellulose by treatment with certain mineral acids or some of their salts. The process is known as *carbonizing*. After a normal emulsion scour, loose wool which is to be carbonized is usually passed through two tanks, lead-lined or of a special stainless steel, similar to scouring bowls, but containing cold dilute sulphuric acid; the wool is then squeezed and passed through a continuous drying machine at a high temperature to concentrate the acid and promote cellulose attack. Two crushing-and-shaking processes are used to pulverize and remove the brittle hydrocellulose from the wool, which is then neutralized by a bath of soda ash solution and double-rinsed in two scouring bowls, and dried (Plate 5).

Rag-carbonizing is explained in Chapter 7 and cloth-carbonizing in Chapter 14.

CHAPTER 7

Rag Pulling, Garnetting and Waste Processing

As already mentioned, in addition to virgin wool the woollen manufacturer also has at his disposal several types of material which have been rejected as waste by other branches of the textile industry. *(N.B.* A certain amount of waste is made at nearly every machine in woollen and worsted processing. However, this is not really wasted in the strict sense of the word, since after treatment it can be put to some other textile use, but its value is usually considerably reduced.)

After suitable treatment these waste materials are blended with virgin wool or with other re-manufactured materials or man-made fibres, or even used alone as explained in Chapter 8. Some of the ways in which such wastes can be converted into a fibrous form suitable for blending, carding and spinning are briefly considered below.

RAGS, SHODDY AND MUNGO

New rags may be woven or knitted materials and consist of clippings from tailors and makers-up, and out-of-date pattern bunches from cloth manufacturers. Old rags include various kinds of discarded garment both knitted and woven (Chapter 4). According to the type of rags some or all of the following sequence of operations can be applied:

1. Sorting by hand, including ripping and seaming, i.e. removal of seams, linings, hooks-and-eyes, buttons, button-holes, etc,
2. Carbonizing, if necessary (*see* Page 40)
3. Shaking—essential after carbonizing,
4. Dusting on machines called *wimseys*—often omitted,
5. Washing, hydro-extracting and drying always follow shaking after wet-carbonizing, but are not applied to uncarbonized rags,
6. Stripping and re-dyeing, if necessary,
7. Blending and oiling,
8. Rag-pulling,
9. Willeying—not for new rags; removes some dirt from shoddy made from rags without a previous shaking,
10. Garnetting—for very hard twisted or thready materials.

Briefly stated, shoddy is derived from knitted goods and unmilled* or very lightly milled woven materials such as worsteds, whereas mungo is usually

* Milling is described in Chapter 14.

shorter in fibre length, being produced from felts and other heavily milled fabrics.

Rag Pulling
The machine is comparatively simple. Fig. 5 shows the direction of movement of
the various parts. The rags are fed by a slow-moving lattice to heavily-weighted
fluted feed rollers, the top one of which is 'coated' with some of the rags. The
surface of the swift is covered with strong metal teeth, which are usually inserted
into wooden lags extending across the surface of the swift. A common type of
general-purpose machine would have forty-eight lags on a forty-inch diameter
swift, with five rows of teeth in each lag and forty-five teeth in each row across
the swift. The cylinder and feed rollers are set a certain distance apart depending
on the type of rag being pulled and on the result desired; the shoddy is judged by
the absence of *rag-bits* and by its stringiness, fibre length, general appearance and
handle. The action of the swift teeth against the rags presented to them by the
feed rollers reduces the rags to a fibrous form and the resultant shoddy or mungo
is discharged from the machine as shown in the diagram. The few rags which for
some reason escape treatment are either deflected by the bit-roller back on to the
feed sheet or pass into the bit-box from which they are removed from time to
time.

Most rag machines are similar in principle and general construction but may
differ slightly in such features as:
1. The method of applying the pressure to the feed rollers,
2. The drive to the feed rollers,
3. The clothing of the swift,
4. Safety appliances such as guards over the feed,
5. The method of driving; variable speed drives with a reversing mechanism for
the feed sheet and feed rollers are available, some operating in a similar manner
to a motor-car gear-box.

The output varies according to the class of rags being pulled and productions
in the order of 100kg/h (220lb/h) may be expected, with higher productions for
softer materials. Present trends are towards wider machines with proportionally
higher outputs. The use of multi-cylinder machines is also now more common,
which may increase the rate of throughput by 50 per cent. Where synthetic fibres
are being processed production rates on modern machines may be considerably
higher.

GARNETTING
Thread waste from the spinning, twisting and warping department, and from
worsted spinning mills, can be converted to a fibrous form by a *Garnett* machine,
named after its originators, P. & C. Garnett Ltd (now Garnett Bywater Ltd). The
machine may be 60, 90, 120 or 150cm (24, 36, 48 or 60 inches) wide and
consists of from one to four cylinders together with other smaller rollers all
covered with a special kind of metallic strip of saw-tooth form (known as garnett
wire) fitted around the entire surface of the cylinders and rollers. The harder

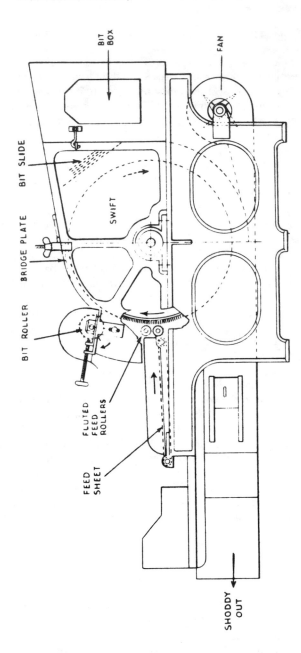

Swift: diameter—102cm (40in); width—46 or 60cm (18 or 24in); speed (rev/min)— 400 for knitted goods, 500—600 for woven cloth, 700 for felts.

FIG.5 Traditional rag-pulling machine (Walker & Smith's)

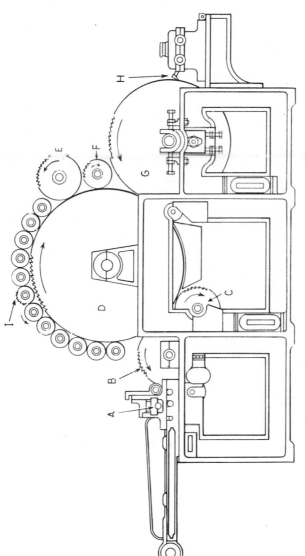

A: Feed rollers B: Licker-in C: Divider D: Swift (or cylinder) E: Fancy F Strippers G: Doffer
H: Doffing comb I: Workers

Class B machine: diameters—76cm (30in) for cylinders; 60cm (24in) for doffers. Cylinder
speeds—140—300rev/min. Production: 7—40kg/h (15—88 lb/h) depending on width, number
of swifts and type of material.

FIG.6 Garnett machine
(Garnet Bywater Ltd)

twisted the material the greater the number of swifts required. Fig. 6 shows the direction of rotation and inclination of the teeth for a one-swift machine. The teeth of the various rollers do not touch each other. Special gauges are supplied by which the rollers are set one to another.

If desired, Garnett machines can be supplied with workers and strippers operating similarly to a carding machine (*see* Chapter 9).

OTHER OPENING AND CLEANING MACHINES
For very hard twisted and knotted materials, such as thrums from weaving, a knot-breaking machine is required before garnetting to avoid damage to the garnett clothing. Other types of dusting and shaking machines are available, some being described in the next chapter.

RAG CARBONIZING
The principle of wool carbonizing was discussed at the end of Chapter 6. Carbonizing is also used for removing cellulosic matter such as cotton threads from rags, but although some rags are *wet* carbonized with sulphuric acid, the acid used for rags is often hydrochloric in the form of a gas. In this *dry* process the rags are treated in a rotating box in a gas chamber, followed by a shaking machine to remove the brittle hydrocellulose so formed. If the rags are to pass direct to pulling without a dyeing process neutralization is necessary after carbonizing.

CHAPTER 8

Blending

The blending department of a woollen mill is concerned with the mixing together of the various raw materials to form a blend, in preparation for carding and spinning. Blending is an essential process in woollen manufacture and is done for one or more of the following reasons:

1. *Uniformity.* It is important that the different lots of material in a blend are mixed together as homogeneously as possible so that the resultant yarn is regular in all its properties*. The blending operations do not effect intimate *fibre-by-fibre* mixing—this is achieved in the subsequent carding process; but blending does prepare the materials for carding by partially opening and mixing the locks of wool and clusters of other fibres which may be present. When the material being processed consists entirely of pure wool without any addition of man-made fibres or cotton, in practice wools of similar quality but of different types are often blended together so as to maintain a standard type of blend. Then if one of the component wools should at any time be unobtainable for some reason† another similar one can be substituted without materially affecting the quality of the whole blend; in short, it is preferable to substitute a part rather than the whole blend. Blending several wools together in this way will also ensure a longer continuous run in processing than can be achieved with one lot of wool.

2. *Price.* In order to make a yarn or fabric at a given cost careful consideration must be given to the price of the raw materials. It is often essential to compromise and mix together suitable materials of different values. Details of costing methods are given in relevant books on textile calculations.

3. *Colour.* Careful blending is essential if a mixture shade of different colours is required. In the case of *solids,* different dyeings of the same colour may differ slightly in shade. By blending them together, irregularities in shade are levelled out.

4. *Special effects.* Some woollen fabrics contain a proportion of man-made fibres, cotton or silk. These other-than-wool materials are mixed with the wool in the blending process. Other effect materials (e.g kemps, knops, etc, *see* Chapter 11) may be added at this stage.

---

*There is much more latitude in the blending of fibres of different lengths and qualities for woollens than for worsteds.

†E.g. delay or shortage of supply from producing countries, exorbitant prices, etc.

5. *Defects.* Blending minimizes slight defects due to previous processes. For example, differences in shade may be evened out. It is also sometimes possible to introduce *a little at a time* slightly inferior material, for example, discoloured, over-scoured or over-dried wool.

6. *Cleaning.* The machines used in a blending room exert a cleaning action on the fibres, but if dusty material is present it is usual and preferable to dust each lot separately prior to blending proper as explained below.

7. *Fibre lubrication.* Woollen yarn manufacture requires the addition of a lubricant to help to minimize fibre breakage in carding and to assist in drafting* in spinning. Therefore a suitable oil is added during blending. The addition of a lubricant also assists in reducing the formation of static electricity†. Some of these oils also help in cloth-finishing (*see* Chapter 14).

MACHINERY IN THE BLENDING DEPARTMENT

There is a variety of machines available; the design and use of any particular machine depend on the amount and kind of work it has to do, which in turn is influenced by the quantity and type of dirt to be removed and the degree of opening required and mixing necessary. Often a particular machine has several different names according to the locality in which it is used.

For preliminary opening and dust removal some sort of *willey* is required, often called a chaker, shake-willey, picker, plucker or teazer. It consists essentially of a chamber containing one or two cylinders about 90cm (36 inches) in diameter with 7.6-cm (3-inch) teeth, rotating at about 500 rev/min. The material can be delivered continuously or retained in the machine for a few seconds before being discharged.

Another cleaning machine is the *self-acting teazer* (wool willow, wool willey, wool opener or devil) which has feed rollers and a single toothed cylinder or swift, 90cm (36 inches) in diameter, rotating at 450 rev/min (Plate 6). Over the swift are two or three 20-cm (8-inch) diameter toothed workers rotating at 30—40 rev/min. The worker teeth enter the spaces between the swift teeth. There may also be a toothed back rail. The action is usually intermittent and impurities are extracted by an air current passing through a grid beneath the swift.

A technique now becoming more popular with the woollen industry is the use of continuous inclined cleaners (Fig. 7). This allows cleaning to be carried out continuously rather than intermittently. Such openers are available in various widths and may process up to 1800kg/h (4000lb/h), depending on conditions. Such cleaners are now manufactured by most makers of woollen processing equipment.

*See Chapter 10.
†Particularly if a specially prepared anti-static agent is incorporated in the lubricant.

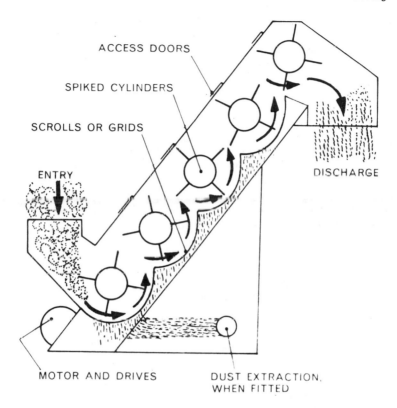

FIG. 7 'Stepblender' inclined cleaner
(Spencer & Halstead Ltd)

A very efficient opening and mixing machine is the *fearnought* (tenterhook willey, cockspur, or—in the West of England—tucker). A common form is shown in Plate 7. It has feed rollers, a swift 122cm (48 inches) diameter rotating at 160—180 rev/min, with two, three or four sets of workers and strippers*. If these are covered with tenterhook teeth and gear-driven, the workers precede the strippers, but if the strippers have straight teeth and high speeds, they precede the workers as in a carding machine. There is a doffer* and often an oiling device, for example

---

* The action of workers, strippers and doffers is explained in Chapter 9.

Walker and Smith 'Rotorspray', which may be above the feed sheet or at the delivery end. Dirt drops through a grid beneath the swift. A fearnought is almost essential in every blending room.

SYSTEMS OF WOOLLEN BLENDING

The arrangement of the machinery and the kind of installation required is largely determined by one or more of the following factors:

1. the types of raw material,
2. the size of the blend,
3. the amount of floor-space available,
4. the capital available initially, and
5. the supply of suitable labour.

   In general there are four main systems of woollen blending available in the United Kingdom, viz:

1. Pile, stack or layer blending,
2. The batch system,
3. Continuous blending,
4. Semi-continuous blending.

Each of these will be considered briefly with its special merits and any possible disadvantages.

Pile, Stack or Layer Blending

This is the oldest method. After separate dusting, thin layers of the various components are assembled one on top of the other in sandwich-formation over a certain floor area and oil is added between the layers by a *lecking-can*. The pile is now broken down by hand at the side from top to bottom in armfuls which are fed to a fearnought or similar opening machine. Each armful should contain some of each component, roughly in the correct proportions. By building-up layers in this way one can ensure that the stack contains the correct proportions of blend with the proper amount of oil added between the layers. Also, if necessary, a very small total weight can be blended. On the other hand a large floor-space is usually required, the method is slow, arduous, costly in labour, intermittent in nature, and the presence of oil makes the work somewhat objectionable to the operative.

   Stacking and fearnoughting are repeated one or more times until a satisfactory mixture is obtained.

The Batch System

In the simplest form the various components are assembled around a hole in the floor and dropped in armfuls down the hole in approximately the correct proportions. An air current carries the material to an opening machine and then, via a fan unit and over-head trunking, to the first blend-bin (Fig. 8 and Plate 8) where a rotary spreader intermixes the stock for either colour-blending or

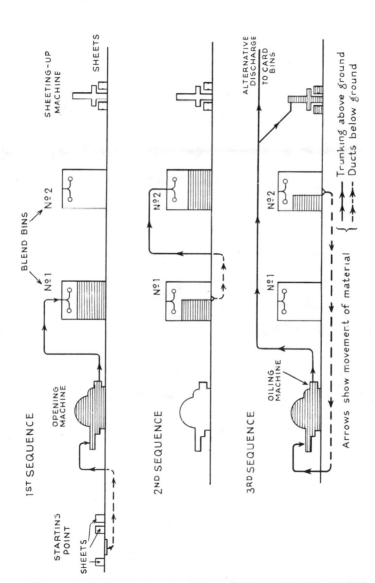

FIG.8 Diagram illustrating the principles of batch blending using a one-machine, two-bin system

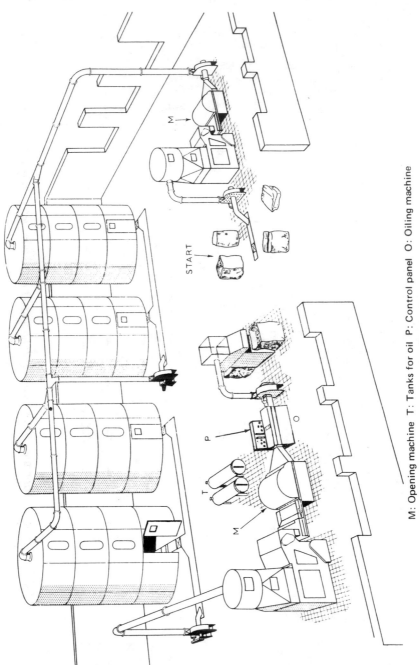

M: Opening machine   T: Tanks for oil   P: Control panel   O: Oiling machine

FIG.9 A modern blending room four-bin, two machine system

(Pneumatic Conveyors (Huddersfield) Ltd)

fibre-mixing. A further bin-to-bin re-mix, via holes in the bin floor and a second
rotary spreader in a second bin, gives the equivalent of a horizontal and vertical
layering, thus ensuring a uniform intermixing of materials. Any number of
intermixings can be carried out in this way.

When sufficiently blended the material may be passed through a final
fearnought and then oiled automatically. In order to ensure an accurate amount
of oil, distributed finely and evenly on the fibres, the 'Spenstead' system uses a
'Vortex' oiler connected to the delivery end of the fearnought, whilst the plant
produced by Pneumatic Conveyors Ltd (Fig. 9) incorporates an 'Atomist' oiler
between the fearnought and the sheeting-up machine. Constant oil-pressure and
viscosity are maintained, ensuring subsequent level oiling*. As an alternative to
the sheeting-up machine, the blend can be discharged direct to storage bins
behind the card sets.

Batch blending is more economical in labour and cleaner for the operative
than the stack method. A one-machine-two-bin circuit (Fig. 8) is usually
capable of handling 9,100–10,900kg (20,000–24,000lb) per 40 hour week
operated by two men. A two-machine-four-bin circuit (Fig. 9) which is more
versatile, handles twice this amount and usually requires only four or five men
for its complete operation. Naturally the actual weight and the number of men
depend on the size and type of blends and to some degree on the layout of the
plant in the available space. Fully-automatic packing machines are also available
which again may reduce the number of men required, if they are considered to
be an economic proposition.

The name Batch System has been given to the above method because the
material is assembled in one *batch* in a bin, transferred as a *batch* to another bin
and so on, and continues to be the most common in use. Sometimes a weighing
device is incorporated at the start of the system.

Continuous Blending

The materials to be blended are first weighed-out into a special weigh-pan in lots
of 45kg (100lb) in their correct proportions. The weigh-pan continuously
delivers these 45kg (100lb) lots into the blending line (Fig. 10). No further
handling need take place until the mixed blend emerges at the end of the plant
for sheeting-up, having been mixed at various stages by blending units and
fearnoughts.

Batch blending is usually regarded as being safer than continuous blending
where a multiplicity of qualities or colours is incorporated in a blend, but the
continuous system has proved extremely successful for the production of blends
for carpet yarns (including tufted carpet yarns) and requires less labour in its
operation. The output from a continuous blending system is entirely dependent
on the output of the slowest machine in the line, generally speaking a fearnought,
and would probably amount to about 680kg/h (1,500lb/h).

---

*Walker & Smith Ltd also claim very efficient oil distribution with their 'Rotorspray' oiler
which operates above the fearnought feed-sheet.

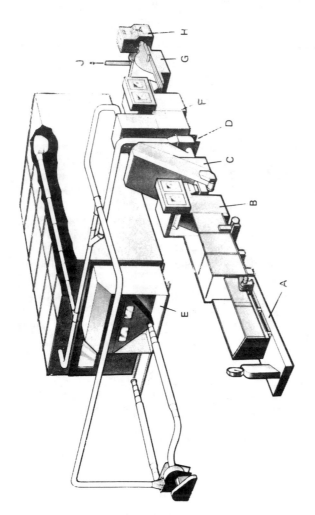

FIG.10 Continuous blending system
(Spencer & Halstead Ltd)

A: Weigh system B: Hopper feed C: Stepblender D: Fan blowing to one of the two bins
E: Automatic bin emptying unit F: Hopper feed G: Opening machine H: 'Vortex' oiling unit
J: Blow to baler or bin

Semi-continuous Blending

This is a combination of the batch and continuous methods. It uses a weigh-pan (or some other form of weighing*) as in continuous blending but the material is then delivered into a bin with a rotary spreader as in the batch system. After a time the feed is stopped and the material is transferred to a second bin and so on. It is claimed that because of the weighing-out and the pulling-down in the bins the semi-continuous system gives better and more accurate mixing than other methods.

Whichever of the mechanical systems is used, care must be taken to clean the inside of the ducting and trunking between the processing of different colours to ensure that no stray clusters of fibres remain which could pass into the following blend. This cleaning problem is one reason why such systems are often considered unsuitable for very small lots.

THE OILING OF BLENDS

Limitations of space preclude a discussion of the types of oil available and the properties required in a wool oil. The amount to be applied depends on the material being processed and on whether part of the blend (e.g. shoddy) has already been oiled. For clean all-wool blends about ten per cent of a good quality oleine should be adequate. A 50/50 oil-in-water emulsion is sometimes preferred, since it is assumed that the emulsion has twice the spreading power of its constituent oil.

Oiling equipment has shown marked advantages in recent years. For example, the 'Spenstead Vortex' oiler now consists of a self-contained unit incorporating its own storage tanks from which the oil or emulsion flows by gravity to a variable-delivery positive volumetric displacement meter passing the pre-set quantity to the atomizer, situated in the centre of a swirling mass of blend discharged by the fearnought into the tangential inlet of the cylindrical oiling chamber. Oil flow is now controlled by the passage of wool along the feed lattice of the fearnought and the result is a simple, foolproof and reliable means of applying the correct quantity of oil in fine spray form to the blend with the minimum possibility of error. Pneumatic Conveyors (Huddersfield) Ltd also make similar devices for the same purpose whilst Walker & Smith Ltd have produced a very effective 'Rotorspray' oiling device for use on the fearnought.

* E.g. Walker & Smith 'Rotamix' blending unit.

CHAPTER 9

Woollen Carding

A carding process is used in the production of most staple yarns, e.g. worsted, woollen, cotton, jute, flax-tow and silk noils; but the machines used for carding the various fibres differ in construction.

In the woollen industry carding follows the blending operations, and after it there is only one further process in yarn manufacture, that is, spinning. Therefore extreme care and vigilance must be exercised in carding for, as will be seen later, the spinning process can do little if anything at all to rectify faults made during carding.

AIMS OF WOOLLEN CARDING

The objects of woollen carding may be stated briefly as:

1. To disentangle the fibres from the different locks of wool or clusters of other fibrous material and, at the same time, continue the work that has already been started in the blending room, by blending together these disentangled fibres so as to produce a mixture of fibres as uniform as possible.

2. Where applicable, to mix together different colours and/or qualities of fibres into a state as homogeneous as possible.

3. To remove from the fibres the maximum amount of impurity; (ancillary devices are usually responsible for making this possible, e.g. 'Peralta' rollers, see later in this Chapter).

4. To produce continuously a web of fibres (extending across the full width of the card), uniform in thickness both across the web and throughout its length.

5. To divide this web into a number of narrow ribbons of fibres, say one hundred, each as uniform as possible in thickness* and width, and to consolidate these ribbons of fibres into cylindrical form called *slubbings* ready for spinning.

In short, woollen carding converts locks or clusters of fibres into a continuous form suitable for spinning into a yarn.

THE WOOLLEN CARD

The machine used to accomplish these objectives consists essentially of a number of large cylinders or swifts and smaller rollers equal in width, usually 150—180cm (60—72 inches) but of various diameters, all covered with a material called card clothing, which consists of a firm foundation of either leather or several layers of fabric-with-rubber or similar material, in which short wires of hardened and tempered mild steel are densely set, to the extent of about 15—110 points or

---

*This is equivalent to saying in more scientific language 'weight per unit length'.

more per square centimetre (100—700 per square inch) according to their position on the machine as explained later.

The carding machine (or *card* as it is usually called) consists of a number of units each composed of a series of rollers comprising a swift with workers and strippers, a doffer and a fancy; the number of such units in a complete machine depends mainly on the type of material being processed, the kind of card clothing used on the card, and the desired result as regards yarn appearance, thickness and quality. Carding machines for various purposes are shown in Figs. 11 and 12. It will be seen that the card is always divided into two or more sections, called scribbler and carder in a two-section machine, and scribbler, intermediate and carder in a three-section card. The object of this division into several sections is to provide better mixing of the fibres by means of the intermediate feeds which connect the sections as explained in detail later.

At the input end of a carding machine the rollers run slowly and have comparatively few but strong wire teeth. As the wool* progresses through the machine the pinning becomes more dense and the wires finer; also the various rollers can be run faster. The relative speeds, direction of revolution and inclination of the wires, together with the distance apart (*setting*) of the adjacent rollers, determine the degree of opening and mixing given to the fibres. Other contributory factors are the sharpness of the wire teeth, the suitability of the wire diameter and the density of pinning in the card clothing for the particular type of wool, the efficiency of the previous wool scouring and drying operations, and the atmospheric conditions prevailing in the carding shed.

Even though everything possible is done to avoid or minimize the breakage of fibres and to maintain fibre length throughout processing, some fibre breakage is inevitable. The reasons for this are beyond the scope of this book.

CARD CLOTHING

The type of card clothing used in the woollen industry varies considerably according to the kind of blend being processed, the composition of the carding set (*see* later in this Chapter), the position in the set of the particular roller to be clothed, and also the personal ideas of the man-in-charge, the carding engineer.

Card clothing may be either *(a)* fillet or *(b)* sheet. The former is in endless strip form varying from 2.5—7.6cm (1—3 inches) in width, usually of vulcanized cloth to hold the teeth firmly. It is wound tightly round the rollers to give an unbroken surface of card teeth as shown in Plate 10. Type *(b)*, which is not now very common, consists of leather sheets of a standard width—usually a 14.3cm (5 5/8in) wide sheet with 12.7cm (5in) covered with teeth—and of a length equal to the width of the card. These sheets are nailed on to the roller side by side *across* the card. Being easy to fix they are often used on the swifts, doffers, workers and fancies of older wooden Yorkshire sets, and if the teeth on part of a roller should become damaged it is necessary to remove and replace only the

---

* For ease of explanation the word 'wool' will be used throughout this chapter, although other fibres may be blended with it.

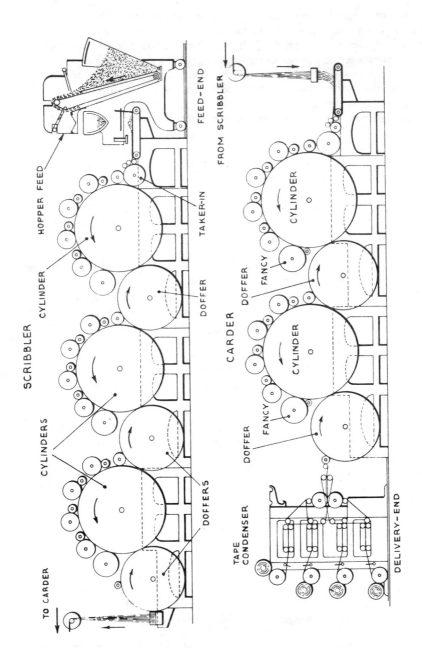

FIG.11 Traditional Yorkshire woollen carding set

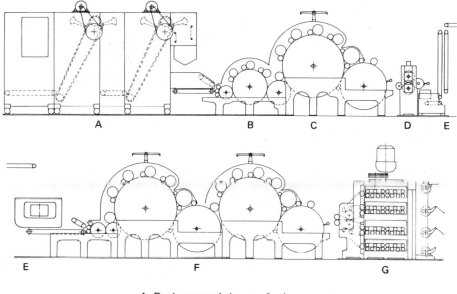

A Dual automatic hopper feed
B 30in breast
C Single-swift scribbler
D 'Crosrol' web purifier
E Intermediate feed
F Two-swift carder
G Four-height tandem rubber tape condenser

FIG.12 Carding set designed specifically for long fibres (details are given in Table 4 on page 67)

(William Tatham Ltd)

damaged sheet, whereas with fillet clothing the whole roller would have to be reclothed. For metal rollers, fillet clothing is popular as it can be wound on tightly without subsequent sagging, and there is an unbroken surface of card teeth whereas sheet clothing necessarily has gaps between the sections of card teeth on adjacent sheets. Sheet clothing is more expensive than fillet.

Many kinds of card clothing are available, with differences in card-wire, shape and angle of teeth, method of setting and type of foundation (Fig.13). For example Continental cards use a special clothing which is thicker and less resilient than normal fillet, and often consists of six layers of cotton and one layer of linen fabric with a layer of thick woollen felt cemented on. The teeth are embedded in this felt up to a point just below the bend of the wire. Semi-continental cards use a similar clothing but with a thinner felt.

In recent years the use of metallic or non-flexible toothed clothing has

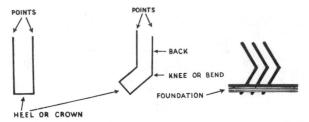

Left: A single staple, front view. Centre: A single staple, side view. Right: Staples in the foundation of card clothing.

FIG.13 Card teeth

become more popular, particularly when processing man-made fibres. This type of clothing resembles saw-teeth and if used will only be found on the main cylinders, namely the breasts and swifts. It was originally used only on Garnetting machines (see Fig.6).

CARDING ACTION

The wire teeth in carding are usually in the form of staples bent at the middle as shown in Fig.13, each staple having two points. The staples pass through the foundation of the card clothing and are held firmly against the metal roller by the tightness of the cloth foundation.

From Figs.11 and 12 it will be seen that at many places on the card two or more rollers are very close to each other. Usually the pairs of adjacent rollers do not actually touch each other but are set by the carding engineer according to the particular type, quality and condition of wool, by means of special thin metal gauges so that they are a known distance apart. Only with the fancy rollers should actual contact be made; the teeth of the fancy rollers mesh into the teeth of the swifts (Fig.14 (v)).

Three kinds of carding action are possible in a woollen card:
 1. Point-of-tooth to point-of-tooth as shown in Fig.14 (i) and (ii),
 2. Point-of-tooth to back-of-tooth (Fig.14 (iii) and (iv)),
 3. Back-of-tooth to back-of-tooth (Fig.14 (v)).

These will now be considered in detail separately:
1. In a carding machine where the rollers are operating with their teeth point-to-point (Fig.14 (i) and (ii)), an opening action occurs or, in technical language, *working* is done. There is in effect a contest between the two rollers for possession of the wool, during which any material held momentarily by either roller is combed through by the teeth of the other roller, resulting in clusters of fibres being disentangled, pulled out or straightened. Two examples of working action are (a) between a swift and a worker (slower-moving) (Fig.14 (i)), and (b) between a swift and a slower-moving doffer as shown in Fig.14 (ii). In both actions the material on the swift is shared by the two rollers. The consequences of this are explained more fully later. There may be twenty or more such places on the card where this working action occurs; these may be progressive in

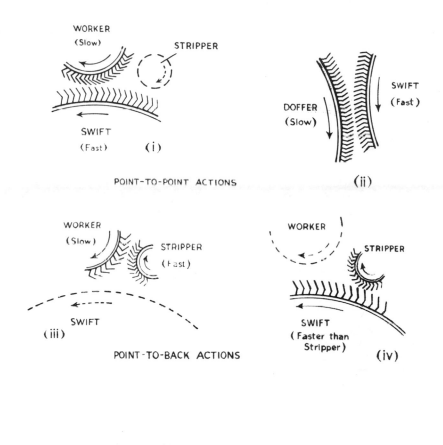

WORKER
(Slow)

STRIPPER

SWIFT
(Fast) **(i)**

POINT-TO-POINT ACTIONS

DOFFER
(Slow)

SWIFT
(Fast)

(ii)

WORKER
(Slow)

STRIPPER
(Fast)

SWIFT

(iii)

POINT-TO-BACK ACTIONS

WORKER

STRIPPER

SWIFT
(Faster than
Stripper)

(iv)

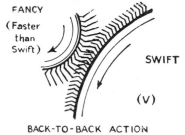

FANCY
(Faster
than
Swift)

SWIFT

(v)

BACK-TO-BACK ACTION

(i) and (ii): Point-to-point (working). (iii) and (iv) Point-to-back (stripping). (v) Back-to-back
(brushing or raising)

FIG. 14 Actions of different pairs of rollers on a woollen card

nature, so that successive places have either quicker speeds or denser pinning or both, with the rollers usually set nearer to each other. This method ensures a gentle and progressive opening of the material with a minimum of fibre breakage and longer life of the card clothing.

2. Fig.14 (iii) demonstrates the *stripping* action where the points of the teeth of the stripper roller approach and pass the backs of the worker teeth. A similar action takes place at (iv) when the points of the teeth of the fast-moving swift approach and pass the backs of the teeth of the slower-moving stripper. In both actions, when wool is present the faster-moving roller strips the fibres held by the teeth of the slower one.

3. The third action which takes place in carding is that of *brushing* or *raising,* when the backs of the teeth of a fast-moving roller brush against the backs of the teeth of a slower moving one, as exemplified by the fancy roller and swift of Fig.14 (v)*. The fibres which have become embedded into the teeth of the swift by several worker—swift actions are now raised again ready to be removed by the doffer (Fig.14 (ii)).

FEEDING THE CARD

Now that the actions possible between the rollers on a woollen card have been considered, the passage of the material from the feed end to the delivery can be discussed in some detail. The modern woollen carding machine is fed automatically by what is known as a *hopper feed.* This device was patented in about 1860 and various refinements have been added from time to time, so that in the modern hopper feed shown in Fig.11 the wool is gradually withdrawn from the hopper box by a spiked lattice moving in contact with the wool. The wool taken upwards in this way passes over the top of the lattice and falls into a *weigh-pan* the width of the card and positioned over the feed sheet. In order to ensure a more or less uniform stream of wool being fed continuously into the machine, a given weight of wool must be dropped from the pan on to the feed sheet at fixed periods of time. This is accomplished by incorporating an adjustable weighing mechanism and a timing device in the pan system, together with means for opening or tipping the pan at the correct time. Several types and makes of hopper feed are available, including a double hopper which is particularly suitable for the carpet, blanket and other coarse-count† sections of the trade (Fig.12).

SCRIBBLING AND CARDING

From the feed lattice the wool passes through a set of intersecting feed rollers to the first part of the card. As previously explained different arrangements are possible but all are similar in action. For example, in Fig.11 the material is taken by the licker-in (or taker-in) from which it is stripped by the angle stripper which in turn is stripped by the swift. Surrounding the upper periphery of the first swift are four sets of workers and strippers followed by a fancy. The actions of

---

*The fancy roller has very flexible teeth.　　　†The term 'count' is explained in Chapter 10.

these various rollers have been considered individually in Fig.14.

Taking them collectively and considering one swift part of the card, the movement of the wool through the machine is as follows. The swift takes the wool upwards from the angle-stripper to the first stripper and worker. The swift —worker action will be considered before that of the stripper; the fibres are separated by the working action, during which encounter the worker takes only *part* of the wool on to its surface whilst the rest goes forward with the swift for further treatment. The fibres taken round the worker are now stripped from it by the stripper (Fig.14 (iii)) which in turn is stripped by the swift (Fig.14 (iv)), and the fibres subsequently join others coming round on the swift from the licker-in. This procedure is repeated with the other workers and strippers, each pair contributing to the aim of distentangling and separating each individual fibre, and also mixing the fibres by the repeated taking up of some fibres by the workers and the re-laying of them on the swift by the stripper—swift action to join and mix with a new set of fibres.

On leaving the fourth set of workers and strippers of the first swift, the wool reaches the fancy. The surface speed of this roller is greater than that of the swift, and, as already explained, the back-to-back action of the two sets of teeth results in the fibres being raised to the surface of the swift clothing in which they were embedded (Fig.14 (v)). With the wool in this new position on the surface the swift meets the doffer which acts in a similar manner to a large worker (Fig.14 (ii)); some of the fibres pass underneath on the doffer surface whilst the remainder go round with the swift for further treatment by the first worker.

The wool on the doffer is transferred to the second swift via the angle-stripper and similar actions take place. Finally the carded fibres are removed from the last doffer of the scribbler by a swiftly oscillating metal comb (about one thousand strokes per minute) in the form of a web*, which is gathered together to form a sliver. The latter is transported to the carder section of the machine by a particular form of intermediate feed known as a Scotch Feed (Fig.11). The different kinds of intermediate feed are explained in the next section of this Chapter. This break in the continuity of the carding machine and the consequent rearrangement of the wool on the carder feed sheet help to mix the fibres (and also the colour, if different shades of fibre are present in the blend), and reduce any variations in the thickness of the stream of fibres both across and along the card due to possible deficiencies or shortcomings in the deliveries from the weigh-pan of the hopper feed.

The fibres then pass through the second part of the machine, the carder, which also consists of swifts and associated rollers. From the last doffer the wool is removed by a stripping roller, or maybe a doffing comb, in the form of a thin web extending across the full width of the machine, say 150cm (60 inches). This web is divided into a number of narrow ribbons of fibres each about 1.25cm (0.5in) wide, the width depending of course on the number of ribbons and the

---

*This may pass through a crushing device as explained at the end of this Chapter.

actual width of the card. This division is accomplished in a *condenser* of which there are several types as described later. The one in Fig.11 is known as a four-height series-tape condenser and it consolidates the hundred ribbons of fibres into cylindrical twistless slubbings which are wound on to four wooden or metal condenser bobbins each of which holds twenty-five slubbings side by side, ready for converting into yarn on a spinning machine.

INTERMEDIATE FEEDS

As previously indicated, the main functions of intermediate feeds are to reduce as much as possible any irregularities in the rate of flow of fibres through the card and to attempt to increase fibre blending, and also uniformity of shade if the blend is coloured.

Several classifications could be adopted for intermediate feeds, but in this book they have been divided into two categories, namely continuous and intermittent. The former includes the Scotch, Apperley, broad-band, straight-fibre and similar types, whilst the Blamire, ball-and-bank and lap-formers are *intermittent* in action—they split up the carding process into distinct operations.

CONTINUOUS FEEDS
Scotch Feed
This is a very popular type because of its simplicity in operation, versatility and convenience for small lots. Two kinds are available—the older type side-draw and the more recent centre-draw. In the side-draw method, the web of fibres coming from the back doffer of the preceding part of the carding engine is deposited on a narrow endless lattice travelling at right-angles to the doffer. A continuous sliver is thus formed, which passes through a pair of metal rollers at the side of the card, up to an overhead lattice, and is then conveyed to the next part of the machine, where it enters a pair of rollers fitted into a carriage moving backwards and forwards across the feed sheet (Fig.11). The speeds of the various lattices are arranged so that there is a minimum of drafting* of the sliver (to avoid breakdown), and the layering of the sliver on the feed sheet is arranged to give a uniform distribution avoiding gaps.

An alternative type of Scotch feed is the centre-draw. In one make, the web from the scribbler doffer is fed on to two leather lattice sheets running to the centre and is thus in the form of a neat flattened band, free from twist and ragged edges which often occur when a side-draw Scotch feed is used. Usually, conveying lattices support the sliver to the next part of the card, this making the device eminently suitable for short-stapled materials and for blends of a weak nature. Another make of centre-draw feed eliminates the lattice after the doffer and uses two cones to support the selvedges of the web and to help to consolidate it into sliver.
Apperley Feed
This type is now very little used, but was at one time very popular in the USA.

*Drafting means drawing out thinner (see Chapter 10).

In principle it is very similar to the side-draw Scotch feed except that the sliver is consolidated by a rotating funnel, and this twisted sliver is laid diagonally on the feed sheet of the next part of the card. The advantage claimed is a better mixing capacity due to the method of entry of the slivers into the next part, but it is not usually recommended before a single part carder. It has been suggested that the twisted form of the sliver may lead to excessive fibre breakage in the next part of the card. Choking of the rotating funnel can be a nuisance with lofty blends.

Parallel-fibre, Straight-fibre, Broad-band and Other Similar Feeds
In one type (made by William Tatham Ltd) the thin web emerging from the previous part of the carding set is combined into a thick, wide sliver by placing layers, one on top of another, on to a horizontal lattice moving slowly in a direction almost at right-angles to the direction of motion of the web. It is possible to combine up to some thirty layers of web; the number can be altered by a simple wheel change. This effects a good mixing and blending and assists in levelling out any hopper irregularities. The delivery of the sliver to the carder is so arranged that the fibres are substantially in the same direction as when they leave the previous doffer in spite of the mixing which has taken place. This sliver is entirely supported throughout its passage from intermediate to carder, and it is claimed that the apparatus is thus suitable for all classes of material, especially blends where the sliver is too weak to support its own weight. The parallel-fibre feed is ideal for securing level effects in coloured mixtures. The mechanism of such a feed is rather complicated in comparison with that of a Scotch (side-draw or centre-draw) feed, but its use is recommended for all types of material.

Most woollen machinery manufacturers, both in this country and abroad, make intermediate feeds, the principles of which are similar to that just described except that in general the layering on the subsequent part of the card is slightly different. Usually, after the many thin layers have been combined on the lower transverse lattice, the composite band of sliver passes upwards between lattices to a height well above the top of the card, and is then laid backwards and forwards on the feed of the succeeding part. The principle of this is shown in Fig.15, and the name *camel-back* is sometimes given to some of these feeds. Several types of straight-fibre broad-band feed, diagonal broad-band feed, and modifications of these are made by British and Continental makers; but all are designed to give a wider and thicker sliver which ensures a better mixing capacity than that given by the Scotch feed, and leads to improved distribution of the fibres over the subsequent feed sheet. In all types the sliver is well supported in its passage from one part of the card to the next (Figs. 11 and 12).

INTERMITTENT FEEDS
Blamire Lap Former
This was specially adapted for very short-fibred material but it is not used today. It is very bulky and cumbersome, since the sliver is supported at all points, but it was once popular in the Morley trade, and is also used in felt manufacture. The

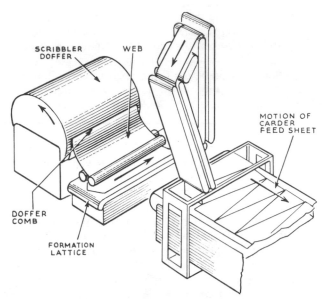

FIG. 15 Principle of broad-band feed
(Reproduced by permission of Wira)

web from the last doffer of the scribbler falls on to an endless lattice which is
moving at the same speed away from the doffer. At the other end of this lattice
the web passes between a pair of tin rollers which deposit it on a lattice
underneath. This lattice is moved bodily on rails to and from the doffer a
distance equal to the width of the carder part. In this way the web is folded over
on to itself some fifty or sixty times to make a thick lap, which is continuously
being wound on to a lap-stick at the end of the lower lattice (and, of course, at
the side of the card). Two or more laps are then fed simultaneously to the
carder to achieve regularity and effect blending and mixing, but unevenness can
arise at the joints of laps.

Ball-and-bank Feed
The Scottish tweed trade often employs three-part carding sets consisting of a
double scribbler with breast, a single intermediate and a double carder with
single-stripper or tape condenser. There may be a ball-and-bank feed (Plate 11)
between the scribbler and intermediate, with a Scotch feed between the
intermediate and carder. Other arrangements are, however, possible. When a
ball-and-bank feed is used the wool from the doffer is drawn to the side, as with
a Scotch feed, but it is then wound on to a wooden bobbin in a special roping or
balling machine. In feeding the next part of the card a four-height creel is used,
accommodating sixty to ninety-six balls. The feed requires considerable attention
and floor space (especially when storage space for the balls is taken into account),

but it can undoubtedly be superior to other types for obtaining uniformity of sliver and intimate mixing, due to the number of *doublings*. It can also be used for 'cobbling in the bank', i.e. making slight adjustments for shade, if the feed is used between the scribbler and intermediate parts with a Scotch feed operating between intermediate and carder parts. In spite of this feed being labour-intensive it still remains popular in parts of the Scottish industry.

Continental-type Lap-drums and Lap-formers

In order to achieve better mixing by doubling on a three-part Continental-type set, a lap-drum may be used after the scribbler, and a lap-former after the intermediate. Although they are seldom, if ever, used in the traditional woollen industry of the United Kingdom, lap-drums are said to be popular in Italy. They appear to be ideal for effectively mixing and blending coloured materials, but there is no *sideways* lapping of the web by traversing at any point (as with a Scotch feed), so extreme care must be taken in laying the laps on the feed sheets.

Lap-formers (Plate 12) are, however, now widely used in the non-woven industry and, as such, are utilised in the manufacture of many fabrics previously woven from conventionally spun woollen threads, e.g. certain blankets and felt-type fabrics.

CONDENSERS

Before condensers were introduced in the early nineteenth century the Slubbing Billy (similar to the 1770 Spinning Jenny, but with a moving spindle rail) was used as a preliminary to spinning.

As already explained, a condenser as used today divides the web of fibres taken from the last swift of the carder into a number of continuous ribbons and then consolidates them into slubbings and winds them on to condenser bobbins ready for converting into a yarn on some form of spinning machine.

There are two distinct methods of condensing, namely:
1. By ring doffers,
2. By tape condensers.

These methods differ in the manner in which the web is split up. The ring type may be further subdivided into single and double ring doffers, whilst tape condensers include series, endless and steel tapes. (Steel tapes are not used in the United Kingdom, so will not be mentioned again.) Each type generally has its own particular uses.

SINGLE RING DOFFER CONDENSER

This was invented in 1821 and is often referred to as the 'single stripper'. It is used in the fine trade for producing very level yarns such as hosiery yarns, and for short wool and 'Angola'* blends of medium count†. The last doffer of the carder is clothed with rings of card clothing, with a small space between one

---

*'Angola'—see Chapter 5.   † Yarn count is explained in Chapter 10.

ring and the next; for example the rings may be 1.9cm (¾in) each with spaces of
0.6cm (¼in). Thus on a 150-cm (60-in) wide card there would be sixty rings of
card clothing producing sixty 'good threads'*. Fibres are removed from the
swift only by the rings of card clothing on the doffer; those fibres that are
adjacent to the spaces on the doffer remain on the swift. Therefore the doffer is
usually given a slow sideways traverse to ensure that the whole of the surface of
the swift is eventually cleared of fibres. Alternatively the workers on the last
swift can be made to traverse from side to side to distribute the fibres across the
surface of the swift, a method that achieves a similar effect.

The individual ribbons of fibres are removed from the doffer by a stripping
mechanism and pass between a pair of oscillating leather aprons which move
simultaneously in two ways: they pass the ribbons of fibres forward and at the
same time they rub each one into a cylindrical form known as a slubbing. There
is no twist in this slubbing—the fibres are merely held together by their own
cohesion aided by the rubbing action. The slubbings are then wound side by
side on to two condenser bobbins.

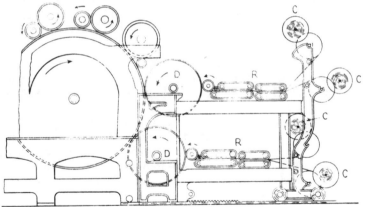

D: 50-cm (20-in) doffers. R: Rubbing leathers. C: Condenser bobbins (four long bobbins or
eight short bobbins).

FIG.16 Double doffer condenser

DOUBLE RING DOFFER CONDENSERS

These were first produced about 1825 and give a larger production than can be
obtained with a single stripper. They are often used for longer-fibred blends and/or
thicker yarns. As shown in Plate 13 and Fig.16 there are two doffers, each clothed
with rings of card clothing so arranged that the rings of one doffer are directly
opposite to the spaces in the other. Thus the fibres that are left on the swift
opposite to the spaces of the top doffer are taken by the rings of the bottom
doffer. Because the top doffer 'gets the first pull' on the fibres of the swift, the

---

* In addition there is at least one waste thread from each side of the card. These are not
  used in case they are uneven in thickness.

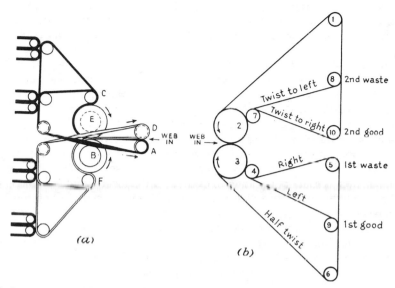

(a) Series tapes: A and D—entry rollers; C and F—pressing rollers; B and E—bottom and top tape cylinders.
(b) Endless tape: The order of threading is 1,2,3,4,5 (1st waste thread), 6,3,2,7,8 (2nd waste thread), 1,2,3,4,9 (1st good thread), 6,3,2,7,10 (2nd good thread) and then repeat 1,2,3, etc.

FIG.17 Threading of tape condensers (four-height)

rings are usually narrower than those on the bottom doffer, since the object is to equalize the weight per unit length of the slubbings from the two doffers. For example, the width may be 2.5cm (1 inch) on the top doffer and 2.7—2.9cm (1 1/16—1 1/8in) on the bottom doffer. Otherwise different doffer-swift settings and/or speeds would be needed. In spite of such precautions, the top doffer usually receives the longest fibres from the blend, and also there are often differences in slubbing count, so many firms keep the condenser bobbins from the top and bottom doffers separate and spin them on different spinning machines.

SERIES TAPE CONDENSER

Tape condensers were evolved in 1861 by Celestine Martin of Verviers. Today the most common type is the series tape that consists essentially of two sets of bands of leather or synthetic material positioned side by side as shown in Fig.17 (a). The bands which pass round the top taking-in roller go to the bottom of the machine and those which pass round the bottom roller go to the top. The web of fibres coming from the last doffer passes between the two rollers and is divided into a large number of narrower webs whose width depends on the width of each tape, which in turn depends on the number of tapes across the machine; if the card is 150cm (60in) wide with one hundred and twenty tapes, each tape will be 1.25cm (0.5in) wide. From the tapes the ribbons of fibres pass between rubbing leathers*, and the slubbings so produced are wound on to condenser bobbins.

ENDLESS TAPE CONDENSER

This is similar in general construction to the condenser just described, but instead of a series of tapes, it has only one long tape which is interlaced around the dividing cylinders (Fig.17 (b)). In its passage through and across the condenser this tape supports every one of the slubbings. With *series* tape condensers difficulties can be experienced owing to differences in tension between individual tapes; a tight tape takes more fibres than a slack one, thus forming a thicker slubbing. The design of the *endless* tape condenser is intended to eliminate this cause of variation but usually differences in slubbing thickness still exist and the use of one type or the other is largely a matter of personal preference.

A 120-thread endless tape condenser on a 180-cm (72-in) machine may require up to 244m (800ft) of tape, so care must be taken to ensure that it is kept in good condition, since if it breaks and 'runs off', a new endless tape has to be re-threaded—an arduous and time-consuming job.

CONDENSERS FOR LARGE-PACKAGE SPINNING

In recent years there has been greatly increased use of the ring-frame for woollen spinning and the demand for large packages† containing up to a kilogram (two pounds) or more of yarn has necessitated wider spindle pitches (or gauges) on frames than were previously used in mule spinning (Chapter 10). To avoid having to *splay out* the slubbings as they come from the condenser bobbin on the spinning frame because of these wider spindle pitches, it is desirable to make wider cheeses of slubbing at the condenser to coincide more closely with the distance between adjacent frame spindles. This has been accomplished by the introduction of two additional types of condenser:

1. The tandem-creel tape condenser,
2. The traversing-creel tape condenser.

In the *tandem-creel condenser,* shown in Plate 14, at each height there are two lines of surface drums at the same level, one behind the other. For 10-cm (4-in) pitch ring-frame spinning up to about 97 tex (20 YSW‡) yarn, there could be four heights, each with two 145-cm (57-in) condenser bobbins one behind the other, fifteen ends per bobbin, and either series or endless tapes. When the bobbins are full those nearest to the operative are changed first, and then the inside ones are lifted over the newly replaced front bobbins.

---

*Usually there are four or six sets according to the number of slubbings produced: e.g. 180 threads would usually require a six-height condenser, 120 threads a four-height.

†The term 'package' is used to cover cops, pirns, bobbins, etc, i.e. all forms of holder for yarn.

‡For YSW see Chapter 10.

When a *traversing-creel* condenser is used, the creel carrying the surface drums is much wider than normal and the thread guides remain stationary while the drums oscillate from side to side. For example in a 180-cm (72-in) card with four-height tape bringing off ninety-six good threads on eight half-length bobbins (twelve threads per bobbin) the cheeses are 12.5cm (5in) wide if the drums are each 150cm (60in) wide; alternatively arrangements can be made for 120-cm (48-in) wide drums to give 10-cm (4-in) cheeses. These figures compare with a maximum cheese width of about 7.5cm (3in) for a condenser *not* equipped with a traversing creel. Obviously the wider cheeses contain more slubbing and they will give a higher efficiency when used on the spinning frame.

To meet the demand for still larger packages giving increased production, an 'internal surface-drum drive' is available to enable condenser bobbins with 28 cm (11 in) diameter flanges to be made on 20-cm (8-in) diameter drums, and to a diameter of 36cm (14in) when fully loaded, thus giving a holding capacity considerably greater than that which would be available with a conventional drive.

THE CHOICE OF CONDENSERS

The length of the fibres, the desired quality of the slubbings and the production requirements primarily govern the type of condenser to be used. The ring system, and particularly the single stripper, is claimed to give greater sliver uniformity because there is no cutting or breaking of the web or robbing of one tape by another as can take place in some tape condensers. The production of the single stripper is low compared with a double doffer or a tape because of the fewer ends of slubbing.

The tape condenser can condense a greater number of finer slubbings than either of the ring doffers; for example 180 ends can be made on a 150-cm (60-in) wide machine whereas a single stripper of similar width would only give about sixty. The tape condenser may be regarded as a general-purpose machine and it is used wherever possible because of its high production.

THE OPERATION OF CARDING SETS

THE COMPOSITION OF WOOLLEN CARDING SETS

The composition of carding sets varies from district to district and from mill to mill. It varies according to:

1. Type of blend,
2. Kind and thickness of yarn required,
3. Locality,
4. Personal preference.

There are differences in:

1. Number of sections in the card (e.g. scribbler, intermediate, carder),
2. Number of swifts per section,
3. Number of workers per swift,
4. Type of intermediate feed,

5. Type of condenser,

6. Kind of card clothing, e.g. sheet, fillet, full-felt, half-felt, etc.

In this book it is only possible to give a brief outline of some common types of machine:

1. The so-called *Yorkshire* set comprising a three-, four- or even five-swift scribbler, scotch feed, two-swift carder, followed by either a tape or a ring-doffer condenser (Fig.11).

2. The *Scottish* set which consists of a two-swift scribbler with breast, ball-and-bank feed, single-swift intermediate, Scotch feed, two-swift carder and either a tape or single-stripper condenser (Plate 11).

3. The *Continental* card, consisting of two parts, the first including a metallic breast, followed by a tape condenser, the intermediate feed usually being some type of broad-band or similar feed (Plate 9).

4. The *semi-continental* set, which is a compromise between 1 and 3 and usually comprises a metallic-breast, a two-swift scribbler, a centre-draw, broad-band or similar feed, a two-swift carder and a tape condenser.

There are, of course, variations and modifications in different districts, and all four types can be found in the West of England.

SPEEDS AND PRODUCTIONS IN WOOLLEN CARDING

Because of the many variable factors outlined earlier it is impossible to be specific about the speeds of the various rollers of a woollen card. However, certain basic relationships exist which may be summarised as follows. The main rollers, i.e. breast and swift, will rotate at speeds varying from 50 to 120 rev/min, a modern continental-type card having the higher speeds. Worker speeds range from 4 to 9 rev/min depending on their size. Strippers rotate at speeds in the order of 200–300 rev/min. Doffer speeds will be approximately 6 rev/min, whilst the surface speed of the fancy would normally be expected to be some 30–40 per cent greater than the surface speed of the swift on which it is acting. Comprehensive data on speeds will be found in some of the references listed in the Bibliography.

Similar problems exist in giving examples of production figures, but again some guidance may be obtained from Table 5 which gives data extracted from *The Wira Textile Data Book.*

AUXILIARY FACTORS IN CARDING

FETTLING AND GRINDING

As carding proceeds, fibres and grease become embedded in the card clothing and at intervals this accumulation of fibres has to be cleared from the card wires. This work is known as *fettling* and involves skill and experience. Special tools are used for the purpose by fettling teams of about four men, and care is necessary to avoid damage to the expensive card clothing. When the card is started up again after fettling, a period of time, say fifteen to twenty minutes, must be allowed for the card clothing to 'fill up' again with fibres. The slubbings

TABLE 4

Details of a Tatham two-part card for processing long fibres—widths 150—250cm (61—97 inches). See Fig.12.

Scribbler	Diameter mm	in	Carder	Diameter mm	in
Breast			*Taker-in & Tummer*		
Feed rollers	84	3 5/16	Feed rollers	84	3 5/16
Taker-in	305	12	Taker-in	305	12
Breast	762	30	Tummer	305	12
Tummer	508	20	*Carder*		
Workers	178	7	Cylinder	1372	54
Strippers	102	4	Doffer	1016	40
Scribbler			Tummer worker,		
Cylinder	1372	54	1st cylinder	203	8
Doffer	1016	40	Angle stripper,		
Tummer worker	152	6	2nd cylinder	152	6
Workers	203	8	Workers	203	8
Strippers	102	4	Strippers	102	4
Fancy	305	12	Fancy	305	12
Stripper under fancy	76	3	Stripper under fancy	76	3
Stripper over fancy	89	3½	Stripper over fancy	89	3½
Stripper over doffer	102	4	Stripper over doffer	102	4
Dick roller	127	5	Dick roller	127	5
Roller under cylinder	76	3	Roller under cylinder	76	3
Web purifier					
Entry roller	152	6			
Pressure rollers	254	10			
Doffer	203	8			

produced during this period are not used for spinning as they are usually 'light in count', that is, thinner than normal. (The material is not entirely wasted; it is pulled up and used again in the blend or fed into the hopper box a *little at a time.)* This disadvantage can be obviated to some extent by the use of the Wira Autocount mentioned later and little waste need be made provided the fibres do not vary much in properties or colours. Vacuum methods of fettling are now also commercially available.

Research has shown[*] that if the fibres are of very much the same diameter but different lengths the card tends to pass forward into the slubbing a predominance of short fibres and to retain the long fibres during this filling-up period. On the other hand with equal fibre lengths and different diameters, coarse fibres are passed forward and the finer ones tend to be retained. Thus

*Journal of the Textile Institute, 1949, p.94.

TABLE 5

Production rate of a woollen carding machine

The production rate of a card is

$$c \cdot r \cdot d \cdot n \cdot \frac{1 \cdot 885}{10^7} \quad kg/h,$$

where: c = slubbing count (tex)
r = rotational speed of the surface drums (rev/min)
d = diameter of drums (mm)
n = number of good threads delivered.

Example
c = 194 tex (10 YSW), r = 30 rev/min, d = 203 mm (8 in), n = 100,

$$\text{production rate} = 194 \times 30 \times 203 \times 100 \times \frac{1 \cdot 885}{10^7} = 22 \cdot 3 \, kg/h \ (= 49 \cdot 1 \, lb/h).$$

Production rate per unit width of woollen card
In comparing production rates of machines of different width it is necessary to allow for the width. This is conveniently done by calculating the production rate per unit width, P. The values tabulated below indicate typical values of P that have been achieved in practice. Factors which can affect the production rate are the number of ends on the condenser and the degree of consolidation required by different blends for different end uses.

Typical values of production rate per unit width of card

| Blend quality | Slubbing count | | Machine width | | Production rate | | P | |
	Tex	YSW	mm	in	kg/h	lb/h	kg/h/cm	lb/h/in
Carpet yarn	390	5	1,830	72	81·6	180	0·45	2·50
	390	5	2,440	96	108·9	240	0·45	2·50
Hosiery yarn (all-wool)	160	12	2,540	100	72·6	160	0·29	1·60
Medium quality wool	215	9	1,525	60	18·1	40	0·12	0·67
	195	10	1,525	60	15·9	35	0·10	0·58
	135	14½	1,525	60	13·6	30	0·09	0·50
	115	17	1,525	60	11·3	25	0·07	0·42
	96	20	1,525	60	9·1	20	0·06	0·33
Wool/nylon/ polyester	160	12	1,525	60	15·9	35	0·10	0·58
Lambswool	96	20	1,525	60	6·8	15	0·04	0·25

Reproduced, by permission, from The Wira Textile Data Book.

there can be a marked 'sorting effect' if a blend consists of (1) long fine fibres together with (2) short coarse fibres, and this can be serious if (1) and (2) are of contrasting colours.

The length of time between fettlings varies according to the type and cleanness of the blend. It may be from a few hours for dirty blends to a week for very clean material. Some firms split the fettling so as to minimize the filling-up effect. For example they fettle the scribbler one day and the carder the next*.

Constant running of the carding machines blunts the points of the teeth to the extent that they eventually become ineffective in teasing apart the fibres without breaking them. The teeth must therefore be sharpened from time to time; emery rollers are used, working lightly against the back of the teeth. This *grinding* operation is skilled work. Smaller rollers such as workers and strippers are lifted out of the machine and treated in a grinding frame, but the swifts and doffers are ground *in situ* on the card.

REMOVAL OF BURRS, HARD THREADS AND OTHER IMPURITIES

The chemical process, carbonizing, has already been explained. In addition, mechanical means are available for crushing any hard, thready or vegetable matter present in a blend. One of the most common mechanisms is the 'Peralta' device introduced in 1937 by Messrs Duesberg-Bosson† of Verviers. More than 10,000 of these units have been supplied throughout the world. One of the latest consists essentially of two precision-ground metal rollers with hydraulic pressure (about 30cm [1ft] in diameter and of card-width) which can be heated and thermostatically controlled to eliminate static and ensure viscosity of the fibre lubricants. The device is placed either *(a)* between the scribbler and the intermediate feed (Fig.12) or *(b)* after the last doffer but one of the scribbler. The web passing between the rollers should be thinner than the material to be crushed out. It is then taken by a doffing roller from which it is removed by a fly-comb. The crushed impurity is dropped from the wool fibres by the actions of the various rollers in later parts of the card.

Other makers, such as Crosrol Ltd of Halifax, and Haigh-Chadwick Ltd of Cleckheaton, supply similar machines with pressure applied either by springs or hydraulically, and with rollers slightly offset (i.e. skew) or slightly convex to give even distribution of pressure. Magnets are usually added to remove ferrous impurities and obviate damage to the rollers, whilst scraper blades are fitted to keep them clean.

WIRA AUTOCOUNT

This is a photo-electric device which (1) continually measures and records the thickness of the web between the last doffer and the tape condenser and (2) adjusts the speed of the doffer and condenser accordingly, in order to ensure

---

*An interesting research project on this topic is described in the Textile Recorder, May, 1960, pp66—8

†Now Houget Duesberg-Bosson.

slubbing levelness. Its use after fettling has already been mentioned. It is of particular use when manufacturing hosiery yarns.

ALTERNATIVE TO CONVENTIONAL WOOLLEN CARDING

Carpet and other relatively thick yarns (including yarns for tufted carpets) are sometimes spun from *slivers* prepared by methods other than woollen carding, and frequently referred to as *semi-worsted* spinning. The essential feature of semi-worsted, as compared to worsted, processing is the omission of combing, together with the associated processes* of intermediate gilling, backwashing and top finishing. The yarns thus produced contain fibres of all lengths, and are much bulkier and lack the leanness and smoothness associated with worsted-spun yarns.

After suitable opening and blending, the first operation in semi-worsted processing is carding. Several types of roller-cards are available including down-striker flax-type cards (the details of which are beyond the scope of this book) or alternatively the more normal wool card. Card productions are in the order of 500kg/hour depending on width and type of card and the material being processed. The second and third stages in the processing sequence utilize high speed intersecting gill boxes*, the first being equipped with an autoleveller unit. The second gill box may well deliver into two cans.

The semi-worsted producer has a range of machines to choose from for the fourth operation, his choice being influenced by the type of material being processed and the character required in the end product. The machines available include:

1. A third high speed gill box.
2. A draw frame* probably incorporating double-apron fibre control in the drafting zone which may deliver the material in either a twisted or twistless form.
3. A draw frame incorporating a caterpillar-type drafting zone.

The final stage in the sequence of processing is that of ring spinning (*see* Chapter 10). Using a double-apron type of fibre control, drafts between 20 and 30 are regularly used. Depending on the end use of the yarn a folding operation may follow.

* An explanation of these process and machines will be found in 'The Worsted Industry'—see Bibliography.

CHAPTER 10

Woollen Spinning

Spinning is a single operation and is designed to convert the slubbings produced by the card into a yarn of a specified degree of fineness and amount of twist.

COUNT OF A YARN

The fineness or diameter of a woollen yarn is indicated by a count number. In the tex count system, now being advocated for universal adoption for *all* yarns of both natural and man-made fibres, the count is the weight in grammes of one kilometre of yarn. For example, if a kilometre of yarn weighs 40 grammes the count is 40 tex.

On the Yorkshire skeins woollen (YSW) count system the count is defined as 'the number of 256-yard hanks (or lengths) in one pound of the particular yarn'. For example, in one pound of 20s YSW yarn there are 20 x 256 = 5,120 yards. Thus the finer the yarn, the higher the count number. There are several other count systems in use in different localities; for example the Galashiels count is the number of 'cuts' of 300 yards in 1½lb, whilst the count in the metric system, often used on the continent of Europe, is the number of kilometres of yarn per kilogram.

For further details the reader is referred to books listed in the Bibliography; additionally, a short conversion table is included at the end of this chapter.

To convert tex to YSW and vice versa the formula used is

$$YSW = \frac{1,938}{\text{tex count}} \quad \text{or tex count} = \frac{1,938}{YSW}$$

In practice the count of a yarn is determined by weighing a short length of the yarn and making a calculation. Because there are 256 drams in a pound and the hank length in the YSW count system is 256 yards, the calculation of count in a woollen mill is easy. It is only necessary to find the number of yards of yarn which weigh a dram.

DRAFT IN WOOLLEN SPINNING

The reduction in thickness of a woollen slubbing, in order to convert it into a yarn with the addition of twist, is termed *drafting.* Draft may be stated numerically as

$$\frac{\text{Weight per unit length of slubbing fed into the machine}}{\text{Weight per unit length of yarn delivered}}$$

or, because the thinner the yarn, the higher the count number,

$$\text{Draft} = \frac{\text{YSW count of yarn}^*}{\text{YSW count of slubbing}}.$$

For example, if a 24s yarn is spun from a 16s slubbing the draft is $\frac{24}{16}$ = 1.5.

The application of draft effects a redisposition of the fibres into a thinner arrangement and this can be achieved either:

1. By passing a sliver, slubbing or roving through two pairs of rotating rollers spaced at an appropriate distance apart with the entry rollers having a slower surface speed than the delivery rollers, or

2. By a revolving inclined spindle drawing out the fibres as it moves away from a pair of rollers holding or slowly delivering the slubbing (*see* Fig.18(a)).

Method 1 is called *roller-drafting* and is used in several machines in worsted and cotton yarn manufacture and also, in a modified form, on the woollen ring-frame; method 2 is *spindle-drafting* and is used in woollen and cotton-waste mule spinning. As will be seen later some twist is inserted during drafting in mule spinning to control fibre movement.

Because of (a) the variation in the length of the fibres in any slubbing delivered from a woollen card and (b) the lack of perfect alignment or orientation of fibres owing to such factors as the penetrating action of the fancy teeth into the swift, the building-up of fibres on the doffer, and the shuffling action of the condenser rubbers, the draft applied in woollen spinning cannot exceed 2, whether the material is being mule-spun or frame-spun. This means that a given length of slubbing cannot be drawn out to more than twice its length if a regular yarn is to result. In fact, 1.5 is a common average draft, as in the numerical example above, where in practical jargon the slubbing is said to be 'condensed at two-thirds of the yarn count'.

The type of fibre influences the amount of draft that can be used. For example, for 'Angola' (a mixture of wool and cotton) and also for low woollen blends, the condensed counts would be about three-quarters or four-fifths of the spun counts, whilst for a very regular good quality wool a draft of almost two may be permissible†. The drafts used in frame spinning are often slightly lower than those for the mule.

---

*Draft can also be expressed as $\frac{\text{tex of slubbing}}{\text{tex of yarn}}$

†When using 'roller-drafting' techniques in cotton or worsted spinning, much higher drafts, in some cases in excess of 100, may be used. This is because of the greater uniformity of fibre length and better fibre alignment, but it results in the yarn spun having different characteristics.

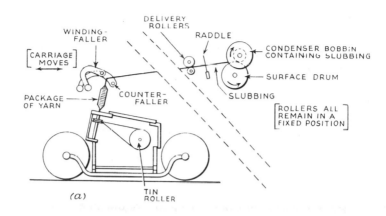

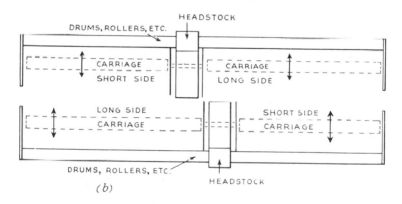

(a) Side elevation of mule (b) Plan of pair of mules

FIG. 18 Woollen mule spinning.

TWIST IN SINGLE WOOLLEN YARNS

Twist plays an important part in any spinning process. Without twist the fibres have very little cohering property. Twist draws the fibres closer together and gives strength and solidity to a yarn; if imposed in small degree it leaves the thread soft, full-handling and open, whilst if a great amount of twist is inserted the yarn becomes very compact, hard and even brittle according to the degree of twist imposed. The amount of twist affects the strength and elasticity of a yarn. Up to a certain point the yarn strength increases with addition of twist, but beyond this point the strength decreases[*]. The degree of twist can affect the

[*] The point varies with the particular yarn and is determined by several factors beyond the scope of this book.

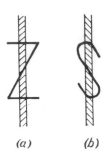

(a) Z-twist   (b) S-twist

(a)   *(b)*   *FIG.19 Twist notation*

design and appearance of a cloth and improve or diminish the lustre of the material by its effect on light reflection. It can also affect the finishing processes and the handle of the cloth (*see* Chapter 14).

In the United Kingdom the amount of twist has traditionally been stated in *turns per inch* (tpi) but the present trend is towards the use of *turns per metre* (turns/m) as used in some other countries. The direction of rotation of the spinning spindle will determine in which way the fibre lie in the yarn. Clockwise rotation gives twist from left to right called Z-twist, whilst anticlockwise rotation gives S-twist (Fig.19). S-twist is usual in woollen spinning, often known as *crossband* (named after a method of driving the spindles), whilst in the twisting process (Chapter 11), when two or more single yarns are twisted or *folded* together, the opposite direction, i.e. Z-twist, is customary in order to give a more balanced yarn. Worsted yarns, on the other hand, have Z-twist in the single and S-twist in the folded yarn.

The amount of twist to be imposed in a yarn cannot always be expressed as a mathematical formula. It must be determined by the amount necessary to give the fibres the required spinning property, plus any further amount required to make it suitable for the purpose for which it is intended, e.g. warp, weft or fancy yarns. The authors have found the formula $\text{tpi} = 5 + \dfrac{\text{YSW}}{3.5}$ useful *as a guide* for spinning twists in all-wool warp yarns up to about 40 YSW count.

For example, 21 YSW yarn would require $5 + \dfrac{21}{3\frac{1}{2}} = 11$ tpi.

This formula may also be stated *(approximately)* as

$$\text{tpi} = 5 \left(1 + \frac{110}{\text{tex}} \right)$$

$$\text{or turns/m} = 200 + 11 \text{ YSW}$$

$$\text{or turns/m} = 200 \left(1 + \frac{110}{\text{tex}} \right)$$

An alternative formula giving similar results is $2.4 \times \sqrt{\text{YSW}}$, which for 21 YSW also gives 11 tpi.

This formula may also be stated *(approximately)* as

$$tpi = \frac{106}{\sqrt{tex}}$$

$$or\ turns/m = 95\sqrt{YSW}$$

$$or\ turns/m = \frac{4200}{\sqrt{tex}}$$

It must be realized however that the type of raw material, its end-use and the spinning performance* must all be borne in mind when deciding on the degree of twist to be imposed in a particular yarn. The use of more twist than is necessary means a loss of production for a given spindle speed. For example, in frame-spinning the rate of production depends directly on the delivery speed of the front rollers, and front roller delivery (metres per minute) = $\frac{rev/min\ of\ spindle}{turns/m}$, so if the twist is increased, the production is reduced for a constant spindle speed.

Twist affects the levelness of a yarn, since in an uneven yarn it tends to settle more in the thinner places than in the thicker places, thus aggravating yarn irregularity.

WOOLLEN SPINNING MACHINERY

There are two main types of machine used for woollen spinning. The older type, the *woollen mule,* is still common in the United Kingdom. Until quite recently it was regarded as more versatile and capable of making yarns which were better and more typically woollen in appearance than yarns made on its competitor, the *ring-frame.* In the early 1960's however, improved ring-frames were introduced by several makers, and many advantages are claimed for these. As a result these are now many more ring-frames than mules used in the woollen industry.

THE WOOLLEN MULE

Mule spinning has been used in the cotton, worsted† and woollen industries, but the woollen mule differs from those used for spinning cotton and worsted yarns in regard to the drafting of the roving or slubbing. Cotton and worsted spinning mules use roller-drafting whilst the woollen mule uses spindle-drafting. It is a complex machine (Plate 15) and, although still popular in the United Kingdom, it is being superseded throughout the world by woollen ring-frames described later.

*For example, number of ends-down (i.e. thread breakages).

†Both cotton and worsted mules are now obsolete. Because of the mules' complex mechanism and lower output they have been replaced by ring-frames.

The mule was probably so named because the first such machine was a cross between the principles employed in Hargreaves' Spinning Jenny and Arkwright's spinning frame. It is unsurpassed for producing full and soft-handling yarns, but it has several disadvantages compared with a spinning frame: it is intermittent in operation, occupies a great deal of floor space, and is complicated in its mechanisms. For many classes of trade it can be, and indeed is being, replaced successfully by woollen ring spinning frames, which are simpler in operation and maintenance, occupy less floor space per unit of output, operate continuously, require less skill in operatives and supervision and produce much greater weights per spindle-hour.

Plate 15 is a photograph of a woollen mule; a full-size machine usually has 300—400 spindles, and mules are arranged in pairs (Fig.18*(b)*). In this book it is impossible even to give a brief description of all the complicated mechanisms incorporated in the machine, but (Fig.18*(a)*) shows the main parts involved in the drafting, twisting and winding-on. In ring-frame spinning these three operations are concurrent but mule spinning is an intermittent process in which the winding-on is separated from the drafting and twisting, and this fact accounts for the mule's low output compared with that of the frame and is also responsible for its structural complexities.

The cycle of movements in mule spinning can be summarized as follows:
1. The condenser bobbins and delivery rollers revolve and deliver slubbing, whilst the carriage moves outwards at a corresponding rate with the spindles rotating at a slow speed in an anticlockwise direction to insert a small amount of S-twist into the slubbing. The faller wire and the counter-faller wire are out of action respectively above and below the slubbing.
2. When the carriage has travelled about two-thirds of its possible outward movement (i.e. about 122cm (48in) of the full 183-cm (72-in) *draw*) the condenser bobbins and the delivery rollers cease to revolve and they do not move again until stage 7. The carriage, however, continues to run outwards and gradually reduces speed; the spindles are still rotating and both the faller wires remain out of action. It is during this movement of the carriage that drafting takes place*; the 122-cm (48-in) length of slubbing which has been delivered by the rollers is drafted into 183cm (72in) of yarn—a draft of 1.5.
3. The carriage stops at the limit of its draw† and the spindles still rotate in the anticlockwise direction but at a much greater speed—up to 5,000 rev/min on some modern mules. For each revolution of a spindle one turn of twist is inserted in the yarn. In order that twist insertion can take place, the spindles are inclined at an angle of about twelve and a half degrees (Fig.18*(a)*) so as to

---

*Successful working depends on obtaining a correct balance between draft and twist. The twist inserted during drafting tends to settle in the thinner places and strengthen them, leaving the thicker places with very little twist. The latter are then drafted and the twist is redistributed: there is thus a continual state of flux.

†In addition to the 183cm (72in) already mentioned, the draw could also be 198 or 213cm (78 or 84in) according to the construction of the particular mule.

allow the yarn to slip over the spindle top as each turn is inserted. Whilst the yarn is being twisted it contracts a little and tightens. Therefore to avoid breaking the yarn during twist insertion the carriage is made to move inwards a few centimetres towards the rollers. This is called *jacking-up* and the inward movement may be up to 20cm (8in) although 2.5—10cm (1—4in) is more usual.

4. When the required amount of twist has been inserted the spindles reverse a few revolutions to unwind the coils of yarn which have become wrapped round the spindle blade, this being known as *backing-off*. The faller and counter-faller wires (sometimes called winding and tensioning wires respectively) come into position ready for winding the yarn on to the cops.

5. The carriage runs in towards the rollers and the yarn is wound on to the cops, being guided by the faller wire and tensioned by the counter-faller. The spindles are rotating in the same direction as when twisting, that is, anticlockwise.

6. The carriage stops at the roller beam and the faller wires are withdrawn.

7. The cycle of operations (1—6) commences once more.

Thus drafting and some of the twisting are performed during the running out of the carriage, and the remainder of the twisting is done whilst the carriage is either stationary at the limit of its draw or during jacking-up, whereas the winding-on is done whilst the carriage is returning towards the rollers. The whole cycle of movements is usually repeated two or three times per minute. The various stages of a complete cycle occupy differing lengths of time according to the particular yarn being spun, but the following percentages give some indication of the relative times: delivery—20 per cent; drafting—27 per cent; twist insertion —30 per cent; backing-off—7 per cent; winding-on—16 per cent.

Perfect timing of the many parts is essential, and the complexity of the mechanisms (Plate 15) together with the low output and great floor space required when compared with spinning frames have influenced the adoption of frames in the newer manufacturing countries and in time will probably result in the total decline of mule spinning in countries which have been regarded as the traditional producers of woollen yarn.

WOOLLEN RING SPINNING FRAMES

There are several makes of spinning frame in use for woollen yarns and although they may differ slightly in detail, they all operate on the same general principles.

Unlike the mule in which the actions are intermittent, the drafting, twisting and winding-on are *continuous* in ring spinning. The slubbing from the condenser bobbin passes between a pair of metal back rollers, the bottom one being fluted and the top one plain and self-weighted, and then over an adjustable deflector-rod to the front rollers (Plate 16) via some form of false twist device (Fig.20). The latter rotates at high speed* and creates a false twist in the slubbing; this is not a *real* twist but a drafting twist to control the fibre movement during the drafting between the back and front rollers which are 46—61cm (1½—2ft) apart. In mule spinning the drafting twist forms part of the actual yarn twist, but in

*About half the rev/min of the spindle.

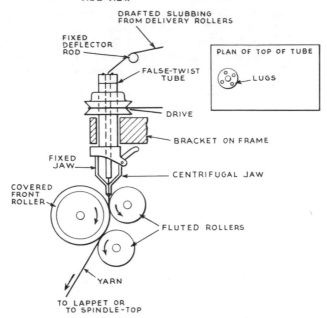

FIG.20 *False-twist tube (centrifugal type) and front rollers of a woollen ring-frame. This diagram shows just one type; several others are available.*

frame spinning it is present during the drafting only; the principle of this is explained elsewhere. In the false twist device shown in Fig.20 the projections at the top of the rotating tube agitate the slubbing as it is being carried round and slipping over them; this is claimed to give fullness to the yarn. Centrifugal force causes the jaws to be held together to grip the material. The yarn leaving the front rollers passes downwards to the ring, as shown in Fig.21(a) which illustrates the *principles* involved in twisting and winding-on. The spindle consists of a steel cylindrical blade supported by and rotating in some type of bolster cup charged with oil which lubricates the spindle. The bolster cup, screwed to the spindle rail, remains stationary. The tube placed firmly on the spindle rotates with it, receiving its motion from a tape drive and whorl. Surrounding each spindle is a flanged metal ring fastened in a ring plate, which during the operation of the frame traverses up and down to distribute the yarn on the tube. On the upper flange of each ring is a small metal clip called a *traveller* which is free to rotate around the ring. The yarn coming from the front rollers is threaded through this traveller and fastened to the bobbin. Winding-on the yarn is accomplished by the traveller lagging behind the rotation of spindle and tube, the yarn thus being drawn on to the tube. The traveller guides the yarn on to the tube and usually in ring spinning the ring and traveller traverse up and down. Normally (e.g. in worsted, cotton and older forms of woollen ring frames, as shown in Fig.21(a)) the yarn *balloons* outwards between the lappet and the traveller, and the tension in the yarn is affected by the air resistance to the yarn, the friction of the ring and traveller, and the centrifugal force set up as the balloon of yarn and the traveller revolve. These in turn are influenced in varying degrees by:

1. Weight and shape of the traveller,
2. Yarn count and twist,
3. Diameter of ring in relation to diameter of tube, and
4. Speed of tube which reacts on the speed of travellers.

However, *collapsed* balloons of the type shown in Fig.21(b) have become increasingly popular for woollen spinning in the last few years (see page 80).

The usual method of altering the tension or drag in ring spinning is by changing the size or weight of the travellers; a heavier traveller imposes a greater tension, whilst a light traveller allows more ballooning. The practical man is accustomed to making changes for different yarns.

Variable-speed drives are sometimes used on ring-frames to counteract the effect on tension of varying winding-on diameter especially when a new set of tubes is being started; a slow speed is needed when the cop diameter is narrowest and the tension highest.

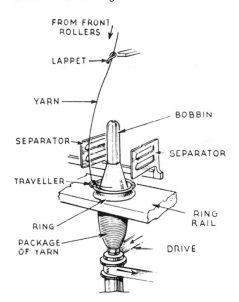

FIG.21(a) *Ring spinning—principles of twisting and winding-on in conventional ring spinning.*

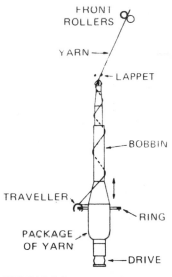

FIG.21(b) *Ring spinning—diagram to illustrate twisting and winding-on in suppressed balloon spinning.*

The twist is inserted by the rotation of the spindle and tube whilst the rollers are delivering the yarn, as the number of turns inserted in the yarn in a given time is equal to the number of revolutions of the balloon. This is less than the number of revolutions made by the tube, as explained above. Thus the twist inserted in ring spinning is slightly variable and depends on the diameter of the bobbin of yarn at the point of winding-on.

In fact, the actual twist at any particular time is given by the formula:

$$\text{turns/m} = \frac{\text{rev/min of tube} - 100\dfrac{\text{front roller delivery (m/min)}}{\text{bobbin circumference (cm)}}}{\text{front roller delivery (m/min)}}$$

There is also an additional slight variation in twist due to the distance between the nip of the front roller and the traveller constantly varying; it is shorter when the ring plate is at the top of its traverse and longer when at the bottom. If the ring rail is run slowly the variations in twist due to this cause are negligible.

MODIFIED SPINDLES ON WOOLLEN RING-FRAMES

Since about 1960 most of the makers of woollen ring-frames have introduced either (i) modified spindles or (ii) attachments fitted to the top of the spindles. The general idea of these is to push the twist up to the delivery roller nip, into the region which normally has less than full twist, thus consolidating the yarn at this critical point (Fig.21(b)). Increased productions and fewer end-breakages are claimed. Plate 17 shows a room of modern woollen ring spinning machines of this type. An extension of the orthodox spindle carries the spool-top which is located at about the position normally occupied by a lappet in the old-type frame. With spool-top spinning the lappet may or may not be dispensed with, the lightweight ceramic spool-top, mounted on ball-bearings, being rotated by the yarn balloon at the speed of the traveller. From the delivery rollers the yarn passes into the top of the spool, emerges at the side and then balloons out and down to the traveller. Threading-up and doffing are simple operations.

Other devices for suppressing or collapsing the yarn balloons are made by several firms, both in the UK and in other countries, but limitation of space in this book does not allow details of the theory involved to be given.

HIGH-SPEED WOOLLEN SPINNING

Modified spindles, balloon control rings, higher traveller velocities[*] and variable-speed driving have enabled increased speeds and productions to be obtained, while large-package spinning allows longer runs and greater lengths of yarn per package, giving fewer knots in later operations, better weaving and a reduction in labour[†].

---

[*] E.g. **36.6m/sec** for a 10-cm diameter ring (120ft/sec for a 4-in ring) with a spindle speed of 7,000 rev/min.

[†] Other advantages of ring-frames, compared with mules, have already been outlined.

MACHINE DETAILS AND SPEEDS

The size and speed of a modern woollen ring spinning frame will vary according to the count of yarn which it is intended to spin. Such frames are in general terms suitable for spinning all counts in the range 970—49 tex (2—40 YSW), at spindle speeds up to a maximum of approximately 8,000 rev/min. Ring diameters will vary from 76—140mm (3—5½in) with lifts from 305—432 mm (12—17in). It may be expected that coarser yarns will be spun on to larger packages prepared on frames utilising the larger ring diameters and the greater lifts. Most machinery makers produce a range of woollen ring spinning frames, each one specifically recommended for a pre-determined count range.

Frames are available single- or double-sided; with a double-sided frame the provision of individual motors for each side permits them to operate independently, thus giving greater flexibility. Numerous other features which can aid efficient production are available, such as: high speed spindles of the suppressed balloon type (Fig.21(b)); self-lubricated or sintered metal rings; tachometers for indicating spindle speeds, roller delivery rates and false-twister tube speeds; a pneumatic system of collecting broken ends (Plate 16); tilting lappet mechanisms to aid doffing; balloon control rings; and variable speed motors. Such aids when correctly used make the woollen ring frame a particularly efficient and versatile spinning machine.

TABLE 6

Tex count conversion table—to or from traditional counts

Tex	YSW*	Galashiels	Metric
49	39.6	50.6	20.4
51	38.0	48.6	19.6
57	34.0	43.5	17.5
61	31.8	40.7	16.4
64	30.3	38.8	15.6
69	28.1	35.9	14.5
75	25.8	33.1	13.3
81	23.9	30.6	12.3
88	22.0	28.2	11.4
97	20.0	25.6	10.3
107	18.1	23.2	9.35
115	16.9	21.6	8.7
125	15.5	19.8	8.0
150	12.9	16.5	6.67
175	11.1	14.2	5.71
215	9.01	11.5	4.65
270	7.18	9.19	3.70
380	5.10	6.53	2.63
480	4.04	5.17	2.08
640	3.03	3.88	1.50

The information in this table has largely been extracted from the Wira Textile Data Book.
*YSW = Yorkshire Skeins Woollen

CHAPTER 11

Twisting and Fancy Yarn Production

For ordinary weaving purposes woollen yarns are frequently used in the single state but, for some special effect or in order to obtain a greater measure of strength than can be reached in single yarns, the latter may be twisted or *folded* together. Carpet yarns and hand-knitting yarns consist of two, three or more single yarns twisted or folded together. Folding is usually done in the reverse direction to spinning; this produces a more balanced structure in the composite yarn. Thus if S-twist is used in the spinning process, Z-twist would be imposed when twisting together two or more of the single yarns*. By different combinations of single and folding twists and by the use of different colours a wide range of yarns can be made to accommodate the requirements of cloth and carpet manufacturers and knitters.

TWISTING MACHINERY
There are three main types of yarn to be considered when deciding on a suitable machine for woollen twisting:
1. Ordinary twofold yarns
2. Threefold and other multifold yarns, and
3. Fancy yarns
    In all of them it is desirable that the breaking of one of the component threads should be the means of stopping the delivery of the other single yarn(s) independently of adjacent spindles, but this is not always possible in practice.

THE OPERATION OF TWISTING
At one time it was quite common for this operation to be done on the mule by replacing the condenser bobbin stands by a creel for holding the packages of single yarn. The delivery rollers were made to revolve all the time that the

---

*If three single 24 YSW yarns are twisted together, the composite yarn is '3-fold 24 skeins' with a resultant yarn count of $24 \div 3 = 8$ YSW. Using the tex system, the three 80 tex yarns would make a composite yarn designated as 80 tex x 3 (or alternatively R240tex/3).

carriage was running out, and twist was inserted during this time and, if necessary, when the carriage was fully out. This method suffered from most of the disadvantages outlined for mule spinning in Chapter 10.

A twisting *frame* (Plate 18) is now almost always used and this is of the ring and traveller type, consisting essentially of a creel for the supply bobbins, a yarn tensioning arrangement, a set of delivery rollers, and spindles. Twofold woollen yarns can be produced on almost any type of twisting frame, or alternatively on a 'fancy doubler'.

To ensure the minimum number of bunch knots in the twisted yarn it is necessary that the frames are fitted with detectors for each of the component single yarns. In some cases, e.g. for carpet yarns, the creel may have facilities to carry up to six feeding bobbins per spindle, and each of the single ends is passed through, and arranged to hold up, a detector. The component threads are then passed forward via the feed rollers. It is of particular importance that a uniform rate of feed is maintained and this may be obtained by the use of three feed rollers, usually one above the other, thus providing a double nip. In some firms use is made of a 'combination twisting frame', which is similar but vertical dolly rollers (as in the *worsted* twofold twister) replace the horizontal rollers. A smooth round yarn is produced because the yarns are not flattened between a roller nip, and they tend to be rolled as they pass round the vertical roller.

If during the twisting operation one of the single ends breaks, the corresponding detector falls and displaces a delicately balanced detector plate, which in turn stops the feed rollers, thereby stopping delivery of the remaining threads. At the same time a lever is moved and stops the spindle rotation by releasing the spindle driving clutch. These movements are instantaneous and leave a sufficient length of yarn behind the rollers to tie up to the particular bobbin. The whole mechanism can be readjusted after tying up the broken end. The exact details of the mechanical operations will, of course, vary in detail on machines made by different manufacturers.

Twisting frames of this type are also indispensable for twofold work where bunch knots must be avoided, because the stop motion permits knots to be tied in the *individual* single yarns. They are also needed for twisting twofold yarns in which the folding twist is in the same direction as the spinning twist, and they are often used for twisting single and multifold yarns together to make fancy yarns (see page 84).

The spindle speeds used for ring twisting frames are determined by the type of yarn, size of ring, and amount of twist being inserted, and may be in the region of 5,000 rev/min. Machine specifications will vary according to the manufacturer; for example James Mackie & Sons Ltd of Belfast produce ring twisting frames of 178 and 254 cm (7in and 10in) pitch having 140mm and 210mm (5½in and 8¼in) diameter rings respectively. The lift in both cases is 585mm (23in) and the bobbin capacities are 2.7kg (6lb) and 5.4kg (12lb) respectively.

Other types of frame are available for producing large packages in order to prolong the time between doffings*. On some of these frames both the spindle and the ring rail traverse so as to give a longer traverse than usual.

FANCY YARNS

Fancy yarns include loop, spiral, cloud, knop, gimp, eccentric, stripe, slub and snarl yarns of different types; there are thousands of possible variations. Many different kinds of single, twofold and multifold yarns may be combined in various ways, incorporating wool, cotton, silk and several of the man-made fibres. Fancy yarns are useful for decorating fabrics and for giving to certain cloths a novel and unusual structure which appeals to some buyers. Some fancy yarns can be made on conventional twisting frames, others require modification to existing machines, whilst special 'fancy twisting frames' are necessary for the more complicated structures. These may include either a mechanical device or in some cases a programmed unit attached to the frame-end, for controlling precisely the delivery of the component yarns, and the relative speeds of twisting.

A special type of knop yarn (otherwise known as knickerbocker, nep or knicker yarn) can be made by spinning slubbing which has been prepared by the woollen carding machine in a special way, i.e. *either* (i) by dropping specially-prepared neps (small hard balls of wool) into the fibres on one of the workers of the last swift of the carder part, from an overhead 'nepping feed', *or* (ii) by incorporating such special neps in the blend and setting the rollers of the carding machine in such a way that these neps are not carded out, but retain their solidity in the condensed slubbing and ultimate yarn.

A detailed description and photographs of various fancy yarns appear in the Textile Institute's book *Textile Terms and Definitions.*

TWO-FOR-ONE TWISTING

Since the publication in 1964 of the first edition of this book the textile industry has seen the much wider use of 'two-for-one' twisting. The idea, patented in 1929, was originally only used for the production of tyre-cord yarns, but the technique may now be successfully applied to the twisting of worsted and certain woollen yarns. As the name suggests, the basic idea is to insert *two* turns of twist into the yarn for only *one* revolution of the spindle. This is achieved by causing the yarn to pass the supply package *twice* during its route to the take-up package, as may be seen from Fig.22. Although the technique enables twist to be inserted at a higher speed it is necessary for the supply package to be previously prepared with the two (or more) component threads, wound side-by-side. This is a separate operation and is known as 'assembly winding'. Two-for-one twisting machines are supplied by several of the world's leading textile machinery makers.

---

*Some firms wind the single yarns on to cheeses or cones (see Chapter 12) before twisting, in order to obtain longer runs without knots.

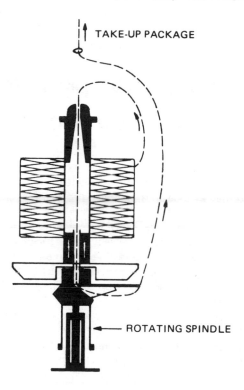

TAKE-UP PACKAGE

ROTATING SPINDLE

FIG. 22 A typical two-for-one spindle assembly.

The supply package is shown positioned on the vertical hollow spindle. The component threads, previously assembled together side-by-side, pass from the periphery of the supply package upwards, and then down the centre of the hollow spindle, and finally out of the base of the unit and upwards to the guide-eye and on to the take-up package (not shown in diagram).

CHAPTER 12

Winding, Warping, Reeling and Yarn Scouring

There are several ways in which a spinner may deliver his yarn to the weaver, carpet manufacturer or knitter. The different forms of delivery are termed yarn *packages* and they include cops, bobbins, tubes, pirns, cheeses, cones, hanks, beams and ball warps.

Cheeses are cylindrical packages of yarn wound on to parallel wooden or paper tubes on a winding frame specially made for this purpose. Very long lengths of yarn can be wound on to cheeses, an advantage when making warps, as explained later. Each cheese of yarn will contain 0.5—1.0kg (1—2lb) of yarn, or even more, with a length of up to maybe 18km (20,000 yards) according to the counts.

Cones are very similar to cheeses but for cones the paper base is of conical shape and the yarn, therefore, retains a conical formation during the building of the package (Plate 19). Yarns for the knitting industry are usually ordered on cones, as this shape of package allows the yarn to be unwound over-end more easily and with less risk of breaking than when built on cheeses.

Paper tubes are used on the spindles in mule spinning and form a cop of yarn weighing about 170g (6oz). When a minimum of 'tare' is required *pin* cops are used in mule spinning; they consist of a paper tube about 5cm (2in) long, and the rest of the yarn is spun on to the bare spindle.

Hanks are made by reeling the yarn on a machine as shown in Plate 20. They can be made up to any predetermined length or weight, either for the hand-knitting trade or as a useful form of package for yarn scouring or dyeing.

Warp threads run the length of a piece of cloth and a warp is made by assembling a great number of ends of yarn side by side on special machines called warping mills, and then transferring the warp so made on to a beam which fits into the loom.

WINDING MACHINES

This operation simply involves the transference of the yarn from one kind of package to another of more suitable type and capable of holding a longer length than the original. Many types of winding machine are available, varying according to the shape of package required, the class and count of the yarn and the use for which it is intended.

REQUIREMENTS

The essential features of winding machines are:

1. A reciprocating guide to distribute the yarn on the package firmly, so that it will not come apart in handling, yet will unwind easily at the next operation.
2. Suitable tensioning devices to regulate the firmness of the package.
3. In some machines a device to clear the yarn of imperfections such as slubs, thick places, knots, etc.
4. An arrangement either to stop the particular spindle or to detach the reciprocating motion from the revolving package if an end breaks, thus avoiding undue rubbing of the yarn which is on the surface of the wound package.

TYPES OF WINDING MACHINE

In winding yarn on to a package, the latter may be rotated:

1. By surface contact with a driving drum or roller, thus giving a constant surface speed of the package.
2. By rotating the package at a constant number of revolutions per minute.
3. By rotating the package at a gradually decreasing speed so that its surface speed remains constant.

Method (1) is common in cheese- and cone-winding machines, a photograph of which is shown in Plate 19, whilst (2) is used in many pirn winding frames. Method (3) requires a variable speed drive and results in a expensive machine.

Fully automatic winding machines are also available. The supply packages are placed in a creel and empty pirns or tubes are fed from a magazine automatically as required, and discharged when full of yarn (Plate 21).

WARPING

Warping refers to the arrangement of a large number of threads in a predetermined order, number and width, parallel to each other on a beam ready for the loom.

The yarn from the spinning or twisting frame may not be of sufficient length for warping purposes, and consequently has to be wound on to cheeses or cones. By combining the contents of several bobbins on to one larger package in this way, frequent stoppages are avoided during warping.

The length of a warp is reckoned in *cuts;* the length of a cut varies according to the district and in West Yorkshire 64m (70yd) is a common length. The warping department is supplied with full instructions as to the number of cuts, threads in the warp, etc. Thus an order may be for 60 cuts (each 64m long) with 3,120 ends to be delivered on 10 weaving beams with flanges set 165cm (65in) apart.

WARPING MACHINES

There are several modern types of machine available for making woollen warps, but in the main they all work on the same principle as far as the building-up of the warp is concerned.

A horizontal warping mill is shown in Plate 22. The staves have inclined planes or ramps at one end against which the warp is built in sections according to the number of threads per unit width, the width of the warp and the number of ends in the creel (Fig.23). In the above examples there are to be 3,120 ends in the warp, so if there are 240 cheeses or cones in the creel, each section of the warp will contain this number of threads. Therefore to complete the warp there will be $3,120 \div 240 = 13$ sections, and each section will occupy a width of 165 13 = 12.7cm (5in).

The ends from the creel, correctly tensioned, are passed through the dents of a reed which serves the purpose of forming a *lease;* that is, putting each thread in a definite relative position as shown in Plate 23 and Fig.23(a). Here the odd numbered threads pass through the dent *A* and the even ones through the short dent *B*. By raising all the odd threads a band *C* can be inserted in the space so formed. Then by lowering the odd threads and raising the even ones another space is formed, and a second band is inserted. This forms a lease which allows the threads to be identified in later processing.

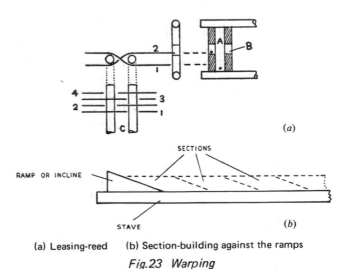

(a) Leasing-reed   (b) Section-building against the ramps

Fig.23 Warping

The threads are next passed through the dents of a contraction or condenser reed for the purpose of crowding the threads to their proper density on the beam and later in the loom. If there are 12 dents to the inch (5 to the centimetre) in this reed the number of ends per dent will be $\dfrac{3,120}{12 \times 65} = 4$. The ends are now passed under and over some measuring rollers and between a section gauge which has been set to the required section width. Finally they are secured to a peg on the underside of one of the staves at the bottom of the ramp.

RUNNING-ON

The building of the first section is accomplished by a mechanism which gradually moves the threads up the inclined plane or ramp on each stave as the mill is revolving (Fig.23(b)). There is a device either to give warning or to stop the mill when the required length has been run on. For example, if six cuts, (that is 380m (420yd)), have to be run on to a mill which is 4.6m (5yd) in circumference, then notification must be given or the mill must be stopped after eighty-four revolutions. The warper then cuts the threads and ties the ends in a special way so that the section will not unwind while later sections are being made.

To build the next section the section guide is moved to the right a distance equal to one section width, and the operation is repeated. This is continued until all the sections have been put on the mill. As shown in Fig.23(b) one section overlaps the previous one, and careful setting and running-on are necessary to avoid a 'ridgy' warp. The creel should also be moved at the same time as the head-stock containing the section guide, rollers and reeds (Plate 22).

BEAMING-OFF

The warp must now be transferred from the warping mill to a weaver's beam ready for the loom. This process is called beaming-off, and the beam is first placed in position at the back of the mill. The threads are fastened to the beam and it is then rotated slowly by power so that the threads are wound on evenly. During beaming-off, the warp is carefully examined and any imperfections are removed and broken threads are repaired.

SIZING OF WARPS

For strong good-quality yarns sizing is unnecessary. It is used mainly for strengthening weak single warp yarns and making them more suitable for weaving, or for the purpose of laying surface fibres in coarse crossbred yarns. The warp is passed through a size-bath and drying chamber in full width. This puts a coat of size on each thread.

REELING AND BUNDLING

A reeling machine (Plate 20) consists of the following parts:

1. A creel for twenty to fifty supply packages.
2. A collapsible cylinder, the circumference consisting of horizontal bars of wood or metal supported by spokes connected to a strong shaft running the full length of the machine.
3. A traversing guide to distribute the yarn in each hank over a space of say 5—8cm (2—3in).
4. A knocking-off device to stop the machine automatically when the predetermined length has been run on to the reel.

After the starting and finishing ends of each reeled hank have been tied together, lease bands are inserted at one or more parts of the hank to prevent entanglement of the yarn in the subsequent processes of scouring, dyeing or rewinding.

When the hanks have been removed from the reel they are made up in bunches of several hanks, and then subsequently assembled into bundles according to the instructions supplied.

YARN SCOURING

Hand-knitting and carpet yarns are usually scoured in hank form, with soap, soda ash and/or other detergents. In general two types of machine are available according to the method of carrying the hanks through the series of scouring bowls: that is, either (1) by tapes or (2) by a brattice, although present trends (1976) are towards the greater use of tape scourers for woollen yarn, as shown in Plate 23.

In *tape* machines the hanks are held firmly between two sets of tapes in their passage through the bowls. There are underwater rollers to ensure adequate immersion of the hanks, but unlike the brattice machine there is only one single passage of the hanks through each bowl.

When a *brattice* scouring machine is used, because of the arrangement of the brattices in the bowls, the hanks pass three times through each bowl; in the first passage they receive a heavy shower of warm detergent liquor (or warm water in later bowls); in the second and third passages they are totally immersed (Fig.24). This type of machine is suitable for scouring all kinds of yarn, but is unequalled for yarns which are heavy in oil or grease, such as carpet yarns, which can be scoured down to one-half per cent final grease content, at a rate of up to 725kg (1,600lb) clean weight per hour on a 1.2m (4ft) wide machine.

After scouring, rinsing and squeezing, the hanks are dried either in a suction-drum dryer or in a single passage dryer suitably equipped for dealing with hanks.

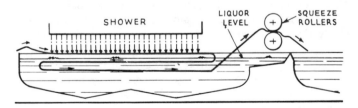

Fig.24   Passage of hanks through a Petrie & McNaught brattice scouring machine

CHAPTER 13

Weaving Woollen Fabrics

PRELIMINARY OPERATIONS

A careful examination of a piece of woven cloth reveals that it is composed of two sets of threads at right-angles to each other. One set is called the *warp* and this is the one that runs throughout the length of a full piece; the other set is called the *weft* and runs across the piece.

Different patterns or designs in a woven cloth are made possible by passing the weft yarns under and over varying numbers of warp threads, and also by the use of different colours and types of yarns. Two such forms of interlacing are shown in detail in Fig.25, where *(a)* is a plain weave in which the weft passes alternately under and over the warp threads, whilst *(b)* is a two-and-two twill which forms the basis of many woollen weaves; *(c)*, *(d)* and *(e)* are other simple examples of the many possible unit weaves which can be used alone or in combination with others according to the design required.

DESIGNING WOOLLEN FABRICS

Briefly stated, the design office in a mill is concerned with the structure of a fabric, the colour, quality and composition of the yarns used in it, the *finish* of the cloth and the costs involved in processing. The designer must bear in mind the limitations of the particular looms at his disposal and his designs should be constructed accordingly (*see* later in this chapter). In fact, besides combining the qualities of a colourist with a high degree of technical ability, the designer must usually have first-hand knowledge of home trade and export requirement; and all this in addition to requiring a good appreciation of costing!

The designer and the blender must work in close co-operation, for the latter is responsible for fulfilling the designer's requirements both as regards the shade and the quality of the components of the yarns to be woven. The designer must also be in constant touch with the dyeing and finishing departments for he is dependent on them for interpreting his requirements and transforming the piece from the loom into a cloth which matches the pattern supplied or approved by the customer.

The method of designing depends on the type of cloth to be produced; simple designs may be worked out directly on special squared paper, called *point-paper,* on which the squares are filled in to show how the threads are to be moved in the loom in order to form the design required in the cloth. From this and other information the quantities of yarn required to make the cloth can be calculated.

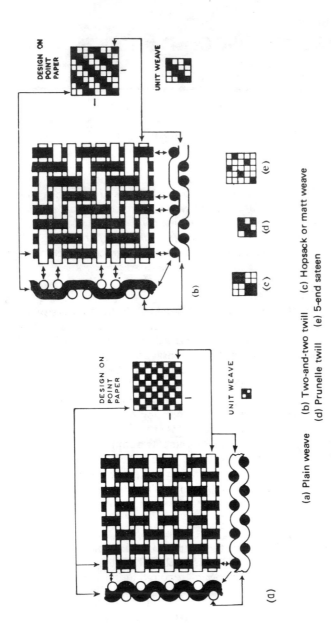

FIG.25 Fabric structures

(a) Plain weave   (b) Two-and-two twill   (c) Hopsack or matt weave
(d) Prunelle twill   (e) 5-end sateen

Generally patterns of a new cloth are first woven by the *pattern weaver* for the firm's travellers to show to their customers and, when orders have been received, full instructions can be passed forward from the design office to the yarn store, the warping department, and later to the drawer-in and the weaver.

DRAWING-IN AND REACHING-IN

When the warp is being prepared for the loom the threads are drawn individually in a specified order through a set of *healds,* such order being called the *draft.* Healds are shown in Fig.26, and consist of a large number of looped cords, shaped wires or flat steel strips with an eye in the centre (called a *mail*), through which a warp yarn can be threaded so that its movement may be controlled during weaving. The healds are held in position in a heald frame and the whole assembly is known as heald shafts, gears or heddles. Fig.26A is a plan view of a set of four healds with the threads drawn-in for a twilled fabric, crosses on the diagram representing the mails (*M* in Fig.26B). After drawing-in, the threads are passed through the dents of a reed; in the example shown there are four threads in a dent.

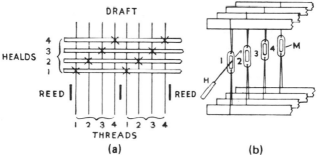

FIG.26 Drawing-in warp threads

The operation of drawing-in is done by mounting the healds in a frame away from the loom with the warp beam suitably positioned. The drawer-in sits in front of the shafts and passes a hook *H* (Fig.26B) through the first mail (*M*) on the left of the first heald shaft. His assistant, called the reacher-in, sits behind the healds and takes the first thread from the lease and places it on the hook. The drawer-in then pulls the hook and thread back through the mail. The second thread from the warp is now drawn through the next mail of the appropriate heald shaft, according to the draft plan with which the drawer-in has been supplied, and so on.

Machines are available which dispense with the services of the reacher-in but for woollen fabrics with only a small number of ends of comparatively thick yarn it is probably as quick to draw-in the ends manually. The Wira Reaching-in Machine is worked solely by the drawer-in, who has the threads presented to him automatically from a magazine mechanism at the rate at which he is drawing them in. The machine thus works at the speed of the drawer-in. After drawing-in, the ends will now be threaded through the reed with a special sley-knife or reed hook.

TWISTING-IN

When a new warp is identical to its predecessor in the loom, there is no need to draw the ends through the healds and reed as just explained; instead the ends of the new warp may be tied or twisted to the corresponding ends of the old warp which are still in the healds and reed in the loom. If performed by hand this twisting-in can be done either in a special frame or in the loom itself. A plan view of the operation is shown in Fig.27 where the yarns are being twisted at *F*.

Twisting-in by hand is time-consuming and there are now on the market several types of automatic knotting machines which can be used on the loom or, if desired, in a frame, but these machines are often regarded as more suitable for worsteds than for woollen yarns.

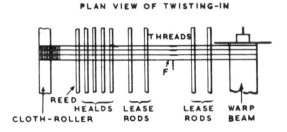

PLAN VIEW OF TWISTING-IN

FIG.27 Twisting-in

APPLYING THE DROP-WIRES

Some looms are fitted with warp-stop motions; each warp thread supports a dropper or *dolly* which falls and causes the loom to be stopped if the particular warp thread should break. As an alternative to dollying a warp by hand, the droppers can also be applied at this stage mechanically by a 'dropper pinning machine'. Two common machines are the Uster and the Wira Dropper Pinning Machines.

When the above processes have been completed the warp is ready for weaving.

THE WEAVING PROCESS

Weaving is the interlacing of two sets of threads at right-angles to each other to form a fabric, as explained earlier. For continuous cloth production a loom (Fig.28) is used, in which the following motions must operate:

1. *Shedding.* This is the term given to the raising of some warp threads and the depression of the remainder so that the weft may be passed through. The opening so formed is called the *shed,* shown in Fig.28. As explained previously

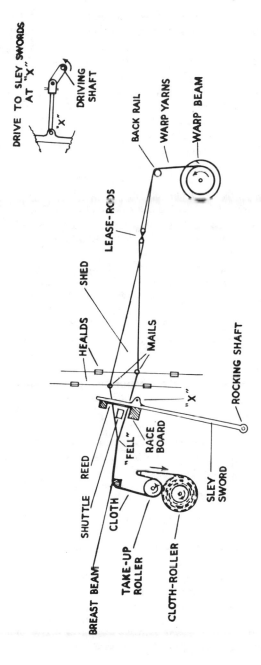

FIG.28 Simplified diagram of a loom to illustrate principles

the warp threads have already been passed through and are controlled by the healds, which in shedding are made to move up and down in some predetermined order.

2. *Picking.* The passage of the weft through the shed is called *picking.* The bobbin, cop or pirn of weft is firmly held in the shuttle (Plate 24) which is projected through the shed by a picking stick and a picker from a shuttle box on one side of the loom to another shuttle box at the opposite side (Fig.29).

3. *Beating-up.* After a weft thread has been laid in the shed it must be pressed hard or beaten-up to the cloth previously formed and a new selection of warp threads made in order to form another shed ready for the insertion of the next pick. This *beating-up* is accomplished by the movement of the reed (Fig.28) which is held in the going-part or sley, pivoted at its base and made to move backwards and forwards at the correct time for beating-up the weft.

4. *Take-up.* Means must be provided for winding up the long length of cloth as it is woven. This is done, directly or indirectly, by means of a *take-up* motion, geared to draw the cloth forward at the same rate as it is woven and wind it on to a cloth roller.

5. *Let-off.* As weaving proceeds the warp threads must be unwound from the beam uniformly in response to the rate at which the cloth is taken up.

In addition to the five motions described there are several mechanisms which may be regarded as auxiliary, in that a loom *could* produce a fabric without them; but they are useful, for example, in stopping the loom in the event of yarn breakages either in warp or weft, or failure of some part of the loom to operate.

By the use of coloured warp and weft yarns, arranged in a definite order, various designs can be woven, and by elaborating the mechanism of the loom as described later, a wide range of fancy woollen fabrics can be produced.

SHEDDING MECHANISMS

There are three main classes of shedding motion in use in the woollen industry and looms are described as tappet, dobby, or Jacquard looms according to the means adopted for forming the shed.

Tappets

The simplest type of loom, and one of the oldest, is the tappet loom as shown in Plate 25. It derives its name from the cams or tappets seen on the lower right of the photograph. These tappets are constructed and operated according to the design required in the cloth so that by means of rods and levers connected to the healds, they cause some warp threads to be raised and others to be depressed, thus forming the shed or opening in the warp threads, for the shuttle to pass through. An auxiliary device, usually incorporating springs fastened to the healds, is required to keep the treadle pulleys in contact with the tappets and after each pick to pull down those heald shafts which have been raised, ready for the formation of another shed.

Tappet looms thus have a very simple shedding mechanism capable of weaving the simpler weave structures. They can be used for weaving a wide range of woollen fabrics such as suitings, serges, gabardines, overcoatings, etc, which do not usually require more than eight healds for their production.

Dobbies

For designs which require more healds than can be conveniently woven by means of tappets a mechanism called a dobby is necessary. Dobbies are available for controlling usually not more than thirty-six heald shafts, although twenty-four and sixteen are probably more common. In structure the loom is somewhat similar to a tappet loom except that instead of tappets there is a dobby, usually fixed to some framework at the opposite end of the loom to the drive as shown in Plate 26. (*N.B.* On some modern low-built or 'topless' looms the dobby is of necessity fitted much lower down on the loom.) Dobbies can be broadly classified into lever dobbies and wheel dobbies, and also further subdivided into positive and negative types according to whether or not the mechanism lowers the heald shafts as well as raises them. The positive dobby is suitable for weaving heavier fabrics, while the negative dobby is used for light- or medium-weight dress goods.

An advantage of the dobby is that no alteration has to be made to the loom mechanism (as in the case of a tappet loom) when the weave pattern is changed, because the design in a dobby loom is regulated by small wooden pegs inserted in lags (or by *bowls* on spindles), or in the case of some modern looms by perforations in a length of stiff paper. The lags are combined in the form of an endless chain which fits over and is driven by a lag cylinder, the rest of the chain hanging down beneath.

Jacquards

Woollen yarns are sometimes woven into figured goods and furnishings. Because of the large number of different threads of warp and weft which feature in a figured or floral design the figuring capacity of a tappet or dobby shedding mechanism is usually insufficient, so a loom fitted with a device called a Jacquard is required[*]. Such a mechanism extends the limit of patterning to make possible hundreds of different warp thread interlacings.

The arrangement for controlling the warp threads *individually* consists of a set of needles acted upon by a pattern card cut with holes and rotated by a *card-cylinder.* The mechanism is situated above the loom as shown in Plate 28, where harness cords will be seen passing downwards to control the individual warp threads in the loom.

There are several types of Jacquard, details of which will be found in more specialised books. Jacquards are sometimes used for weaving patterned blankets of the type shown in Plate 34. An important use of Jacquards is for pattern weaving in the fancy trade

[*]First perfected in France in 1790 by Joseph Marie Jacquard and first used in England about 1830.

INSERTION OF WEFT

The object of picking is to drive the shuttle across the loom (usually by means of a picking stick and a picker) without any jerk or jar, at such a velocity that it will land in the shuttle box at the other side of the loom, being arrested by the friction of the *swell* and the *check*. There are many types of picking mechanism in use, but only the most common will be mentioned here.

Firstly, picking may by *overpick* or *underpick* type. This means that the picking stick (which drives the picker in the shuttle box, in order to propel the shuttle from one side of the loom to the other) is situated above the level of the cloth being woven as shown in Plate 25 and Fig.29(a), or mainly below it as shown in Plates 26 & 27 and Fig.29(b) and (c). Overpick is generally suitable for lighter looms whilst underpick is used on heavier looms.

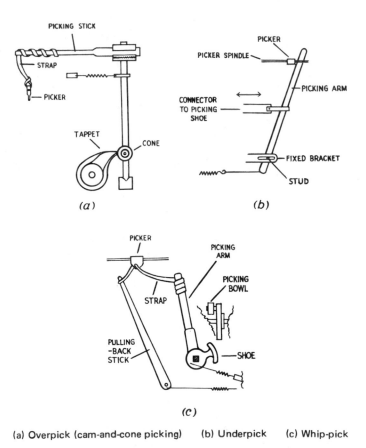

(a) Overpick (cam-and-cone picking)   (b) Underpick   (c) Whip-pick

Fig.29 Some different forms of picking

Secondly, an underpick motion may be either *whip-pick* or of the *pushing* type. The difference lies in the method of moving the picking stick. In the whip-pick it has a strap attached to it as shown in Fig.29(c) which pulls the picker with a whip-like action to propel the shuttle. In the other type the picker is *pushed* against the shuttle by the picking stick itself (Fig.29(b)).

Thirdly, there are different methods of moving the picking stick. An overpick loom may use a *cam* or tappet which revolves once every two picks and actuates a *cone* fixed near the base of the vertical shaft on which the picking stick is fixed (Fig.29(a)). This is known as *cam-and-cone* picking. Another method of picking uses a *bowl* (circular metal piece) which strikes a *shoe* attached to the bottom of the picking stick in order to cause the picker to be moved (Fig.29(c)).

Picking may be made to take place alternately from the left- and right-hand sides of the loom (called *plain* picking) or it can be controlled to pick from either side as required, this being known as *pick-at-will*. The latter method has the advantage that when used in conjunction with multiple shuttle-boxes at *both* sides of the loom it is possible to use several shuttles. This permits:
1. The weaving of cloths with several differently coloured weft yarns, thus extending the range of fancy patterned structures.
2. The use of 'fancy' yarns (*see* Chapter 11) in a fabric along with orthodox yarns.
3. The mixing of weft yarns of the same lot to minimise any possible irregularity, which could cause barriness or other shade faults in the fabric.

The tappet loom of Plate 25 has one shuttle box at each end so is only capable of plain weaving with a single shuttle, whereas the dobby looms shown in Plates 26 & 27 have four boxes at each side in order to provide greater versatility and give the designer scope for very fancy colour-patterning.

Box-motions can be divided into two main classes:
1. The rising or drop box motion, commonly made with two or four boxes at each side of the loom.
2. The circular box motion used on quick-running lighter looms.
The woollen trade often uses type (1).

There have been many attempts to replace the shuttle by other methods of weft insertion but the only ones which have so far been taken up to any extent by the woollen and worsted trade are the Sulzer weaving machine and rapier looms. In these looms the weft is fed from cones at one side of the loom. Late in 1975 a prominent authority summarised the present situation of shuttleless weaving by stating that only 7 per cent of the world's looms were shuttleless, whilst in UK the percentage was higher, 8 percent of the total of 120,000 looms being of this type. He suggested that throughout the world half the shuttleless looms were of the rapier type, although in the UK this figure was only 20 per cent, but as twenty-two of the world's textile machinery makers now made this type of loom it could reasonably be expected that these figures would increase.

The Sulzer Weaving Machine

Small carriers about 9cm (3.5in) long and weighing about 43g (1.5oz) grip the weft yarn and take it through the shed, and on reaching the other side of the loom they drop on to a conveyor which carries them back to the side of the loom from which they were originally propelled. Fig.30 indicates the working principle of the Sulzer machine, and Plate 29 is a photograph of one of the latest models developed for the woollen and worsted trades. Two- and four-colour systems are available and Sulzer machines can operate at more than twice the speed of conventional looms of corresponding reed widths (*see* later in this chapter).

It should be pointed out that because every pick of weft in a Sulzer loom is severed at each side of the loom and the excess is tucked into the edge of the cloth (Fig.30(g)), the sett and weave at the selvedge must be modified so that the edges of the cloth are not so thick as to cause difficulties in finishing, yet are sufficiently strong and balanced to process efficiently.

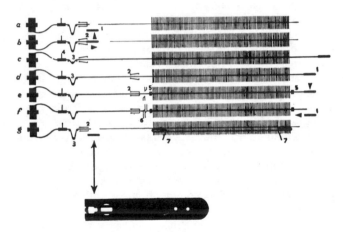

Fig.30 Sulzer weaving machine.

Principle of weft-insertion system:

(a) Shuttle 1 moves into the picking position.

(b) Shuttle-feeder 2 opens after the shuttle has gripped the end of the weft-thread held ready for it.

(c) The thread is drawn through the shed by the shuttle, with thread-tensioner 3 and weft-brake 4 acting to reduce stress on the thread at the moment of picking.

(d) Shuttle 1 is pushed back inside the receiving-unit housing, whilst the tensioner 3 holds the thread lightly stretched; at the same time feeder 2 moves close to the edge of the cloth.

(e) Feeder 2 grips the thread whilst the selvedge grippers 5 hold the weft at both sides of the cloth.

(f) The thread is severed by scissors 6 and released by shuttle 1 inside the receiving-unit housing; the shuttle is then ejected on to the conveyor which carries it outside the shed back to the picking position.

(g) The thread has been beaten up by the reed; the needles 7 tuck the thread ends into the next shed (tucked selvedge); the end of the thread freed by the return of the shuttle feeder 2 has been taken up by the thread-tensioner 3; the next shuttle is brought into the picking position.

The rapier loom

Fig.31 shows diagramatically how the weft is inserted in one type of rapier loom. Looms of this type (Plate 30) are manufactured by several machine makers and, as might be anticipated, differences in detail exist between their various products. Many of the advantages claimed for shuttleless weaving are common to both the rapier and Sulzer machines. Similarly the comments made regarding the selvedge of cloth woven on a Sulzer machine are equally applicable to rapier weaving.

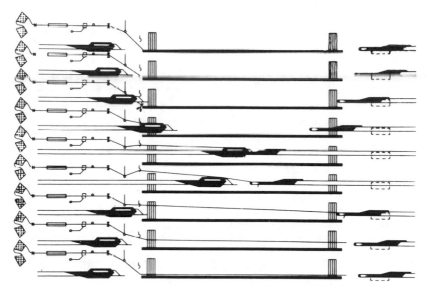

Fig.31 Diagrammatic representation of typical weft transfer cycle on a rapier loom. (Nuovo Pignone. UK agent: A.E. Aspinall Ltd)

BEATING-UP

This is common to all types of weaving; immediately a pick of weft has been passed through the shed it is pressed by the reed hard up to the cloth previously formed. The reed is fixed in the sley or going part as shown in Fig.28, where it will be seen that in addition to beating-up the weft, the sley has to provide a *race* for the shuttle to travel across. The sley requires a quick movement for the beat-up in its front position and a slower movement at the back of its stroke when the shuttle is travelling across the race-board. This motion is obtained from a crank and connecting rod attached at X to the sley (Fig.28). As in all other motions of the loom very accurate timing is essential.

The reed itself fulfils several functions. It controls the number of warp threads per inch and consequently the width of the warp in the loom, and it spaces the threads uniformly. Besides beating-up each pick of weft it also supports the back of the shuttle as it traverses the sley.

TAKE-UP MOTIONS

The cloth must be drawn forward a definite distance each time a pick of weft has been inserted. The type of take-up motion is determined by the type of cloth being woven and the uniformity of thickness of the weft. For very heavily-wefted goods, and for fabrics with weft of varying thickness as in the low woollen trade, a negative take-up motion is used. This is controlled by the tension of the warp, the thickness of the weft at the fell of the cloth and, in some cases, by the adjustment of auxiliary weights on the motion itself; it is driven by the movement of the sley. However, if the weft is very regular as in most worsteds, the take-up roller can be made to rotate continuously or to move the cloth forward a *definite distance* after each pick; such a take-up motion is said to be *positive.*

Modern positive take-up motions employ a friction roller with a covering such as perforated tin, emery or rubber to grip the cloth. This is gear-driven either from a ratchet and pawl operated from the sley (intermittent motion), or by a worm wheel mechanism which gives a continuous and constant-speed rotary movement to the friction roller. Change wheels are incorporated in the gear system so that alterations may easily be made when changing the loom to a cloth with a different number of picks per unit length. The roller on to which the cloth is eventually wound may be driven by a system of gear wheels or by frictional contact with the friction roller as shown in Plates 25 and 26.

LETTING-OFF THE WARP

Tensioning the warp is a very important factor in weaving. The strength and extensibility of the yarn should be carefully considered. If the warp is too slack the threads will not be sufficiently separated in the shedding, with the result that they may be broken, or passed over instead of under by the weft so that the outcome is imperfect cloth. Slackness can also produce other types of fault which may vary according to the structure of the cloth.

Letting-off the warp at the correct rate is also of much importance and it should be performed uniformly with the taking-up of the cloth. The many methods at present available for doing this are too numerous to describe here, and it must be sufficient to say that in the majority of cases they are arranged to hold the beam in such a manner as to keep the warp tight during shedding, but let it off in response to the rate at which the cloth is taken up. There are both the so-called negative and positive let-off motions.

AUTOMATIC WEAVING

In 1894 the first really automatic looms were put into operation in America, and the British Northrop Loom Co Ltd* was founded eight years later to make automatic looms. Today there are many different kinds and makes of automatic loom operating in almost every textile manufacturing country in the world. The essence of automatic weaving is that the weaver need no longer watch the

---

*The style of the company was changed to British Northrop Ltd in 1958.

packages of weft in the shuttles and, when each one is almost empty, stop the loom and replenish the weft. Instead the loom is fitted with a magazine or battery either of full pirns, or shuttles filled with weft (*see* Plates 24, 31 & 32). A mechanism on the loom detects when the weft supply in the operating shuttle is running out and, according to the type of automatic loom in use, it causes either a full shuttle to take the place of the nearly empty one, or the almost spent pirn to be pushed out of the shuttle and *immediately* replaced by a full one without stopping the operation of the loom.

In addition to the mechanisms for weft replenishment, an automatic warp-stop motion knocks-off the loom in the event of a warp thread breaking between the beam and the healds, whilst a weft-fork motion stops the loom if the weft is missing or broken in the shed (Plate 31). Thus more looms per weaver are possible; for example where a weaver can 'mind' one or two ordinary woollen looms, four to six automatics per weaver are possible.

There are many different designs of mechanism for replenishing the weft supply automatically but a detailed explanation is beyond the scope of this book.

The following advantages have been claimed for automatic weaving:
1. Automatic weaving increases the production per operative.
2. Mental and physical strain can be eliminated.
3. Continuous production of more and better cloth is maintained.
4. The production of cloth is scientifically controlled.
5. Cheaper production results.
6. The earning capacity of the operative is increased.
7. The working conditions in the weave room are improved.

It is emphasized that automatic weaving is not merely the installation of automatic looms in the place of 'ordinary' looms. 'It is a system of thought, management and production. It involves not only new automatic weaving machinery, but in many cases modern high-speed automatic preparation and other ancillary machinery. It may also demand changes in sales policy and marketing techniques'*.

AUXILIARY MECHANISMS

Warp-stop motions have already been mentioned in regard to automatic weaving. They can also be fitted to non-automatic looms, and when used in conjunction with a weft feeler motion (which senses when the weft is running out in the shuttle) they make the weaving semi-automatic in the sense that the weaver need no longer be on the alert for the weft running out or for breakages in the warp threads at the back of the loom between the warp beam and the healds. A dropper or dolly is placed on each warp thread, and if a thread breaks the corresponding dropper falls and actuates a mechanism whereby the loom is stopped either by electrical or by mechanical means.

Other auxiliary devices designed both to save time and labour in the weaving shed and also to assist in the prevention of faults and damage in the fabric or to

*Automatic Weaving—The Northrop System (British Northrop Ltd, 1962)

the loom include temples (which keep the fabric stretched to the proper width as it is woven), warp protector motions, selvedge motions, pick-finding devices and heald-levelling mechanisms. For further details textbooks should be consulted.

SPEED OF WEAVING

The rate at which a loom operates is quoted in picks per minute (ppm) and depends on such factors as the type of loom, kind of fabric, quality of yarn and the conditions of running. In general the wider the cloth in the loom, the slower the loom must be run. For example, many dobby looms operate at speeds of 95—110 ppm for reed spaces of about 230cm (90in). Higher speeds such as 130ppm are claimed for the Dobcross 'HK' loom (Plate 27) and the Hattersley 'Standard' loom when fitted with the 'Shirley' dobby, as well as for some of the more recently introduced automatic looms such as the Saurer, whilst the Sulzer weaving machine can operate at nearly double this speed with 216cm (85in) useful reed space.

As an example of the rate of production of cloth, if a loom runs at 105ppm, and the efficiency is 75 per cent, then for a cloth with 38 picks of weft per inch the number of yards of cloth woven per 40-hour week would be

$$\frac{105 \times 60 \times 75 \times 40}{38 \times 36 \times 100} = 138\text{yd (126m) or nearly 2 cuts.}$$

LOOM-TUNING

It will be realised from the foregoing account that the loom is a complicated piece of machinery, and the various mechanisms included in it require careful adjustments so that the five main motions of shedding, picking, beating-up, letting-off the warp, and taking-up the woven fabric, together with the auxiliary mechanisms and accessories, are all in perfect synchronism.

There is no one set of rules for weaving the vast variety of fabrics produced in the woollen industry, and the experience and skill of the loom tuner, foreman and shed manager play a great part in the setting and timing of the various parts of the loom according to the requirements of the fabric to be woven.

CHAPTER 14

Woollen Finishing

When a fabric leaves the loom it is far from being in a suitable state for making into garments or other commodities. It contains imperfections due to various causes such as, for example, breakages of warp or weft threads in weaving, oil added in blending to facilitate the carding and drafting of the fibres, dirt picked up in spinning and weaving, and other defects which have arisen in previous processes. Woven fabrics are therefore first inspected by the *taker-in* or *percher* who specializes in detecting faults. This operation is known as *perching* and consists of passing the piece full-width over rollers or bars suspended from the ceiling and examining it in a good light for imperfections. Faults that cannot be mended are marked with string at the edge or list of the piece, whilst those to be dealt with in the mending room are indicated by chalk. At this stage the pieces are also measured, weighed and numbered for future reference.

BURLING, KNOTTING AND MENDING
The burler takes out any thick places and draws knots to the back of the piece. The mender sews in all threads of both warp and weft which have been left out or broken during weaving, and repairs holes and bad places. Mending is therefore a highly skilled job requiring good eyesight and colour perception, and also a precise knowledge of the weave or design of the cloth. It can also be done during and near the end of the finishing sequence, according to the routine adopted by the particular firm.

FINISHING ROUTINES
The number and sequence of operations in finishing woollens vary according to such factors as:
1. The type and quality of the raw materials used in making the yarn.
2. The type and structure of the fabric.
3. The result required in the finished cloth.
The order of the processing often differs from mill to mill, and in order to cover the vast variety of cloths made by woollen mills, a number of different finishing routines is necessary. Some cloths require a considerable amount of processing, whilst others can be finished with comparatively few operations. Some common finishing processes used for *woollens* are briefly outlined below, followed at the end of the Chapter by suggested routines for a few selected cloths.

SCOURING

This is usually the first process in finishing woollens*, the object being to remove processing oils added in blending (Chapter 8) and dirt picked up during manufacture. Most woollen cloths are scoured in rope form in a dolly scouring machine (Fig. 32), about four 65-m (70-yd) pieces together if a 1.8-m (6-ft) wide machine is used for medium-weight suitings and similar clothst. Soda ash (sodium carbonate) and soap are the usual agents used, and when soap is used the process is said to be an emulsification scour. Many woollen cloths, however, contain added processing oils with a fairly high content of free fatty acid. These cloths may often be scoured satisfactorily with a saponification scour, using soda ash alone, when a soap is formed by the reaction of the fatty acid and the alkali.

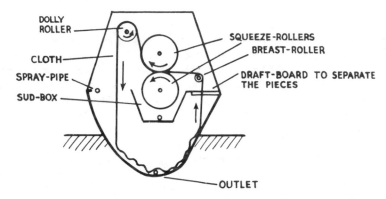

FIG.32 Principles of rope scouring machine or dolly.

The water for scouring should be soft, or, if it is hard, it should be softened to avoid precipitation and waste of soap. Synthetic detergents are sometimes used in place of soap and/or soda ash, especially if the water is hard. The scouring liquor is used at room temperature, about 20 gallons (90 litres), i.e. 200 lb (90kg), at the correct strength for the particular requirements, to every 100 lb (45kg) of cloth, this being termed a 2-to-1 liquor ratio. After running at about 82–100m/min (90–110yd/min) for an appropriate time, for example about half an hour for a Saxony‡ suiting, the pieces are thoroughly washed-off in warm water which is gradually cooled down, the dirty liquor being discharged from the machine via the sud-box. A two-bath scour may be necessary for very dirty fabrics.

*Sometimes a preliminary 'setting' process is required to prevent distortion or curling of the cloth in subsequent scouring and dyeing, but this is more frequent for worsteds than for woollens.

t'Open-width' machines may be used for cloths which crease badly in rope-scouring.

‡See footnote on page 113.

MILLING

This process is used extensively in the woollen industry to bring about a change
in the handle and appearance of the fabric. It is sometimes referred to by its
older names of *felting* or *fulling* (Chapter 2). Milling involves relative motion and
friction between the wool fibres which have been wetted out and swollen,
usually in a suitable soap solution. The cloth is consolidated and given *cover,* the
weave structure being concealed or made less distinct to a degree determined by
the amount of milling given. At the same time there is a decrease in width and
length*; for example a Saxony or fancy tweed piece may be 173cm (68in) wide
in the loom but only 145cm (57in) after milling, and 142—147cm (56—58in)
completely finished, weighing 500-530g/m (16—17oz/yd). A dress-faced cloth
from West Yorkshire may be made with 37—40 ends and picks per inch of 96 tex
(20 YSW) yarn, set about 274cm (108in) wide in the loom with a length of
65m (70yd) but after final milling the width would be 147cm (58in) and the
length 53m (58yd) giving a *finished* weight of 745—810g/running metre (24—26
oz/running yard) at a width of 142cm (56in).

In a milling machine (Fig. 33) heat, moisture, pressure and cloth speed can
all be controlled and varied to give a wide range of effects. Some cloths are only
lightly milled to improve their handle, whilst others, such as meltons and
billiard cloths, are given a lengthy milling which solidifies and shrinks them.

Primitive milling machines have been mentioned in Chapter 2, but although
fulling stocks are still sometimes used for specific purposes†, modern milling
machines are of the rotary type shown in Fig. 33. A milling machine takes one
piece (approx. 65—90m, i.e. 70—100yd) of cloth which is threaded through the
machine several times in rope form‡. It passes through (a) a draft board to
separate the strands of the rope of cloth‡, (b) a throat to bunch it, (c) a pair of
squeeze-rollers of wood or special composition and (d) a spout with a weighted
lid which is forced upwards at its outer end by the cloth as it accumulates in it,
until the build-up of cloth finally forces itself through the spout. The weight on
the lid and the pressure between the rollers can be altered and controlled;
usually the greater the pressure between the rollers the greater is the shrinkage in
width of the cloth, whilst the greater the weight on the lid, the greater is the
shrinkage in length. Measurements are taken from time to time during the
running of the piece so that the cloth can be milled to the correct dimensions of
length and width.

There are three main methods of milling:

1. *Soap milling* directly after scouring, the most common method.

---

*Tests on a number of pieces given a 'standard woollen finish' gave average results, for
  shrinkage, of 10 per cent in length and 20 per cent in width, with a loss in weight of 20 per
  cent in finishing.

†Chiefly in the felt-making trade and for hosiery.

‡A piece may be processed double-, treble- or four-'draft' etc.

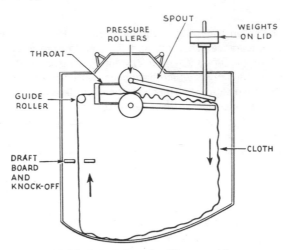

FIG.33 Principles of milling machine.

2. *Grease milling* which is done before scouring by passing the greasy cloth through a soda ash solution and then milling it, followed by scouring and washing off.

3. *Acid milling,* in which the scoured cloth is impregnated with acetic or sulphuric acid, hydro-extracted (*see* below) and then milled and finally washed-off, perhaps with a prior neutralizing treatment.

Each method has its own merits and disadvantages dependent on the type of cloth and the finish required. Briefly stated, compared with soap milling, grease milling effects a saving in labour, it is useful for low-grade fancy tweeds and low quality meltons, but it is not recommended for *very* dirty fabric, whereas acid milling is cheaper, quicker and it may give a stronger cloth, but the handle is harder. Cloths for army greatcoats are often acid-milled.

There is also a 'combined scouring and milling machine' in which the cloth is first scoured and then milled and washed off. This machine is claimed to be capable of dealing with a wide range of cloths and to save time by eliminating the transfer of the cloth from scouring to milling and back again to washing-off in the scouring machine.

During milling the piece should be neither too wet nor too dry; if the latter, there will be excessive flocking and a poorly-milled cloth. After milling, the piece must be thoroughly washed-off in a scouring machine in warm water (gradually cooled down) so that no soap or alkali remains; otherwise in piece-dyeing uneven dyeing may result.

CLOTH DRYING

Excess water can now be removed by mangling and hydro-extraction which expels water from the cloth centrifugally in a machine similar to a domestic spin-dryer but larger—up to 180cm (72in) diameter. A *hydro-extractor* consists of a circular perforated cage mounted on a vertical shaft enclosed within a steel casing. The cage is loaded uniformly with cloth, the lid is closed and the machine is run for five to ten minutes at 700—1,000rev/min until the moisture content is considerably reduced. As an alternative, *suction-slot* dryers, operating on full-width pieces, are gaining in popularity.

Drying is completed in a *tentering machine* (Plate 33). At the same time creases are removed and the cloth is straightened by being attached at the lists to two parallel chains fitted with pins, and dried under tension (Plate 33). In the tenter the cloth passes through the machine from top to bottom in a number of horizontal layers; a 'three-bay twelve-layer' machine holds about 73m (80yd) of cloth. The drying system is often a combination of radiation from steam-heated pipes and hot-air circulation by means of fans. Instrumentation and electrical equipment as shown in Plate 33 ensure accurate control of temperature, speed, width and moisture content of the delivered cloth. The piece will normally be tentered a few inches greater than the finished width required; the actual amount depends on the type of cloth and the succeeding processes.

RAISING*

This process is done to develop a pile or layer of protruding fibres on the surface of a cloth for the purpose of:
1. Obtaining a fibrous effect,
2. Increasing the softness or fullness of handle,
3. Concealing the threads or making the weave effect less distinct, and/or
4. Subduing the colours.

Raising was originally done by hand, by using teazles set in a holder but in later years they were fitted on to the surface of a horizontal, cylindrical machine called a teazle-gig. In a present-day gig the piece is passed, as many times as required, over a 100-cm (40-in) diameter teazle-covered cylinder rotating at about 150rev/min in which the arc of contact of the cloth with the cylinder surface is adjustable. Teazle-gigs are often used for *drawn* or *laid* pile that is raised wet with the surface fibres combed in one direction, as in billiard cloths, beavers and doeskins.

Another type of raising machine, which is more common today, is the card-wire raising machine or 'Moser' (Plate 34) named after Edward Moser of Alsace, who invented it in 1884. The machine is clothed with a special fillet card-clothing (*see* Chapter 9). There are both single-action and double-action machines, the latter having considerable variation in raising-power and being suitable for heavy woollen cloths. The direction of movement of the cloth, the cylinder and the card-teeth are shown in Fig. 34 for both machines.

---

*In the USA this process is called 'napping', but in the UK napping is an entirely different process to produce special effects.

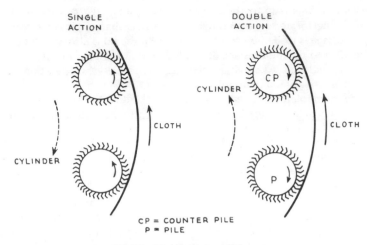

Fig.34 *Cloth raising action.*

The type of pile produced depends on many factors including:
1. Speed of cloth*,
2. Speeds of cylinder and rollers,
3. Setting of rollers to cloth and condition of card-teeth,
4. Number of passages of cloth through the machine,
5. Weave, nature and previous treatment of cloth,
6. Quality of wool,
7. Conditions of raising, e.g. wet or dry.

Fine wools usually give a closer pile than coarse qualities, whilst for a *laid* pile as in doeskins, beavers, superfines and billiard cloths, the fabric would be raised wet. In double-action machines a maximum of raising is obtained when the counter-pile rollers run fast and the pile rollers run slowly. It should be remembered that raising is a somewhat vicious treatment and weakens the cloth, especially weft-ways.

A considerable amount of research has been done and is continuing on the various aspects of raising.

STEAMING AND BRUSHING

The object of this process is essentially to lift up the loose fibres of warp and weft yarns so that they may be removed by the cropping machine to obtain a clear finish†. The brushing machine, as its name implies, consists essentially of one or two horizontally mounted rotating brushing rollers which are adjustable to the cloth passing over them, preceded by a *steam box*. The two

*Speeds up to 46m/min (50yd/min) are claimed for modern machines.

†In a process known as 'dry beating' the cloth is first steamed and then raised dry on a teazle-gig to lift the pile and prepare it for cutting (see page 111).

ends of the piece are sewn together and the cloth is passed round the machine until the desired effect is obtained.

CUTTING OR CROPPING

When required, this process improves the appearance of a woollen cloth by removing fibrous material from the surface. The severity of the process is governed by the type of finish required. Cutting machines are shown in Plate 35 and the principle of the action of the cutting parts is given in Fig.35. The essential features are:

1. The cutting cylinder similar to a lawn-mower,
2. The ledger blade (both (1) and (2) being positioned in a headstock) and
3. The bed over which the cloth passes.

There are also drawing rollers to pull the piece through the machine, a setting-up roller and several guide and tension mechanisms. The flocks shorn from the cloth are removed by a suction device. Very accurate setting and speeding of the various parts are essential to avoid excessive or uneven cutting and damage to the cloth such as holes. Cutting machines are made to operate at cloth speeds up to 46m/min (50yd/min). They can be supplied with any number of cylinders to give the desired number of cuts on the face and on the back of the piece as required for the particular finish and type of fabric. For example, a four-blade machine is made which gives one back and three face cuts.

FIG.35 Principles of the cutting parts of a cutting machine.

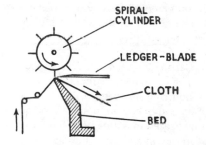

DRY BLOWING

Some woollens are *blown* in order to flatten the cloth and give it solidity and firmness, or sometimes to impart lustre. The blowing machine shown in Plate 36 consists principally of two 60-cm (24-in) diameter perforated metal rollers through which steam can be blown. The cloth is wound together with a special type of cotton wrapper around one of these two rollers, and steam is blown through it for an appropriate time. After air has been sucked through until the roll of cloth is cold it is then transferred to the second roller and treated in the same way except that the end of the piece which was originally outside is now on the inside. This procedure gives more uniform results than would be obtained with a single treatment. The piece is now run out of the machine, and at the same time another piece can be fed on to the first blowing cylinder.

DEWING OR DAMPING

Frequently it is necessary to add moisture to a cloth in order to restore its natural moisture content (or condition). There are various ways of putting moisture into a piece, and the usual machine for doing this consists *either* of nozzles from which water is blown by pressure as a fine spray on to the face of the moving piece, *or* of a brush revolving at high speed in a self-filling trough of water, thus throwing drops of water on to the piece as it passes by. Superior results are claimed for a more recent device which passes the piece between two accurately turned squeeze rollers, the lower of which runs partly submerged in a trough of water containing a wetting agent. A controlled steaming arrangement can be incorporated in the machine.

Whatever system of dewing is used, the piece should afterwards be allowed to stand overnight in cuttle form, that is, loose transverse folds open-width, so that the moisture may be absorbed evenly.

POTTING

This process is used to give a high lustre to face-cloths. The piece is wound on to a roller, placed in a tank of slightly acidic water (acetic acid) and given three or four treatments, each lasting maybe ten hours, at up to 80°C (180°F). Raising may be done between the treatments.

PIECE CARBONIZING

Carbonizing is often done in piece-form rather than as loose wool because:
1. The quality of the wool is thus preserved throughout carding, spinning and weaving, and
2. Piece-carbonizing is a relatively cheap process.
    Carbonizing is often done by commission firms.
    The principles are much the same as for wool carbonizing (Chapter 6). When carbonizing is necessary the cloth is impregnated with an acid solution, squeezed, dried and baked; in modern processing all this is done in full-width. The piece is now beaten in a type of milling machine, neutralized and rinsed. Care must be exercised at all stages. Fabrics made from blends of wool and cotton or man-made fibres must not, of course, be carbonized. Opinions vary as to the position of the carbonizing process in the finishing routine. Some firms prefer it before dyeing because carbonizing a dyed piece may alter its shade. Others maintain that carbonizing a piece directly after scouring may affect the subsequent milling properties and cause uneven dyeing. Carbonizing after milling is convenient for many cloths.

PRESSING

With the object of presenting the cloth in merchantable form the piece is pressed to consolidate the cloth, straighten it and give it an attractive appearance or lustre. According to the finish required, pressing can be done hot or cold. A good woollen suiting would probably be pressed warm, then steamed face and back according to the condition required, followed by *cold flatting* (pressing) and cuttling (final folding). The pressing of high-class cloths is usually done in large hydraulically operated machines in which the cloth (after folding list to list with the face of the cloth inside) is placed by hand in layers between cardboard press papers and pressure is applied, or alternatively it is pressed full-width between press papers interleaved between folds of the cloth by hand. Whichever process is used, it is repeated after the position of the press-papers has been changed, the object being to press those portions of the cloth which were previously not treated, because they were at the edges of the paper. The original method of heating was by hot iron plates, but today electrically heated press-papers are available.

Quicker results may be obtained by use of a *rotary press,* in which the cloth is passed full-width between a heated cylinder and a curved metal bed. This machine, however, is rather severe in action, gives a somewhat 'boardy' handle and excessive lustre, and it tends to stretch the cloth lengthways. A cooling and conditioning machine is usually used after the rotary press.

A continuous pressing machine using press papers is also available.

LONDON SHRINKING

In addition to the processes described above, high quality fabrics may be subjected to a process called London shrinking, which is usually done by firms who specialize in the work. In this process the cloth is thoroughly moistened and then allowed to dry naturally in the absence of tension, to allow the strains imposed during the many stages of manufacture to dissipate. It then requires re-pressing without the introduction of any further strains.

Dimensional stability can also be obtained by a process called *sponging,* popular in the USA. In this, the fabric is fully relaxed by steaming and allowed to dry without tension. The character and handle of the cloth, imparted by preceding finishing treatments, may be affected however, but—as with London shrinking—cloths treated in this way should not shrink during garment-making, for example, in Hoffman pressing.

A FEW FINISHING ROUTINES FOR WOOLLENS

There are many types of woollen fabric, each requiring its own finishing routine, but a detailed description is beyond the scope of this book. In recent years, too, great progress has been made in the industrial application of processes for moth-proofing, shower-proofing and permanent-pleating, and also in the use of foam-backs. A few suggested routines are now given; it is assumed that the cloths have first been perched, measured, numbered, weighed, knotted and mended. It must be emphasized, however, that the method of obtaining a certain finish will probably vary from firm to firm.

Saxony* and High-class Tweeds. Scour; mill to desired cover and width; wash-off well (a combined scouring and milling machine could be used for all

---

*Saxony—a high quality fabric made chiefly from merino wool spun on the woollen system. (The name for fabrics made on the worsted system from merino wool is Botany).

these operations (page 108); hydro-extract; tenter; steam and brush; cut to pattern face and back; blow both ends in, pressing first if lustre is desired; steam and allow to lie; press warm; steam; cold press (cold flat).

Fancy Cheviots*. As Saxony up to cutting; then brush and steam; damp and stand; press warm; steam face lightly.

Velour. Scour; raise face and back if necessary (usually for lower qualities) both ends up; mill; wash-off; moser; dry; tenter; brush; cut level; dye; wash-off; moser both ends up (but if a dress-face is required use a teazle-gig and raise-wet); dry and tenter; steam and brush; cut; press warm with little pressure; steam-off. (A shorter routine may be used for lower-grade material.)

Wool-dyed Melton. Scour; mill for density and cover, but not for width, reversing several times; wash-off thoroughly; maybe 'full' in the stocks; pass through a trough of hot water and wind on roller, and allow to stand twelve hours or more; tenter; steam and brush; cut level on face and back; mill to width; wash-off; hydro-extract; tenter; press; pot twice at $71°-80°C$ $(160°-180°F)$ reversing; dry; tenter; steam and brush; cut to required smartness; blow both ends in; damp and stand; press warm; steam; cold press.

Blankets, Medium Grade. Scour; mill; wash-off; carbonize; *either* (i) dye *or* (ii) neutralize and bleach† if for whites or pastel shades which are to be bleached before dyeing; hydro-extract; tenter; damp and leave overnight; raise damp on teazle-gig or moser; dry; tenter; cut; steam; cut into blanket lengths; whip or sew-on edges.

Dress-face Finish. (This type of finish is applied to billiard cloths, doeskins, beavers, superfines, pilots, venetians and buckskins, which may be of different fabric structures and vary slightly in finishing treatment, but all are given a lustrous surface by reason of the pile being laid wet in one direction in raising.) Scour; mill for density and cover; wash-off; wet-dress on teazle-gig, both sides, both ends in; tenter; dry-beat; cut level; repeat dry-beating and cutting as necessary; wet and dress the face one way on the gig; tenter; dry-dress and cut level, repeating as required; press; pot at $71°-80°C$ $(160°-180°F)$ four or maybe six times, dressing-wet on the gig between each boil; brush and steam; cut level if necessary; damp and leave overnight; press warm and complete with cold-pressing.

A range of booklets and samples representative of the woollen and worsted industries may be purchased from the British Wool Marketing Board, Oak Mills, Station Road, Clayton, Bradford, BD14 6JD.

---

*Cheviot—a fabric made from crossbred or similar qualities of wool spun on the woollen system. (The term 'crossbred worsted fabric' is used for worsteds made from such wool qualities.)

†Peroxide bleaching is often preferred to sulphur stoving, as the effect is more permanent.

CHAPTER 15

Dyeing

Only a brief outline will be given of some methods of dyeing used in the woollen industry, and the reader who requires further information, such as details of specific dyestuffs and their suitability for different fibres, is referred to the Bibliography.

Many of the dyes used for wool are salts of organic colour acids and are known as acid dyes, being sold by a number of dyestuff manufacturers under various trade names. Faster dyed shades are obtained by what are known as mordant dyes, which require chrome to produce a fast chemical combination of dyestuff and wool. When acid or mordant dyes are used and also with a later development known as pre-metallized (or metal complex) dyes, the process is fairly straight-forward, and the material is entered wet into the dye-bath containing a calculated amount of dyestuff and the necessary assistants at a moderate temperature. This liquor is gradually raised to the boil and dyeing is continued gently for about another hour, after which the shade is compared with the standard pattern. If necessary, additions of dyestuffs are made and further boiling is continued until the material does match the pattern. Rinsing follows, first in hot and then in cold water, and the material is then dried.

In addition to acid dyes and chrome dyes, use is also made of indigo. This process is known as vat-dyeing and necessitates a different and more complicated procedure but gives blue shades which are very fast to washing and to light.

DYEING IN WOOLLEN MANUFACTURE

The stage at which the material can be dyed depends chiefly on the nature of the ultimate cloth and on the degree of fastness required. For woollens it is possible to dye wool (i) in the loose state, (ii) as yarn or (iii) in the piece. Rags can also be dyed, but the method is similar to loose wool dyeing and details will be found in specialized books.

Loose Wool Dyeing

At one time open dye-vats were used universally with the wool 'poled' manually in the steam-heated dye-liquor. Modern methods use machines in which the heated dye-liquor is circulated through the wool by a pump or propeller; reversal of liquor-flow is usually possible. The wool is held in some type of perforated container positioned within a stainless-steel outer vat. This facilitates emptying the machine after dyeing, for the container and wool can be hoisted out of the vat and unloaded away from the machine. Fig. 36 shows this together with a modern method of drying the wool.

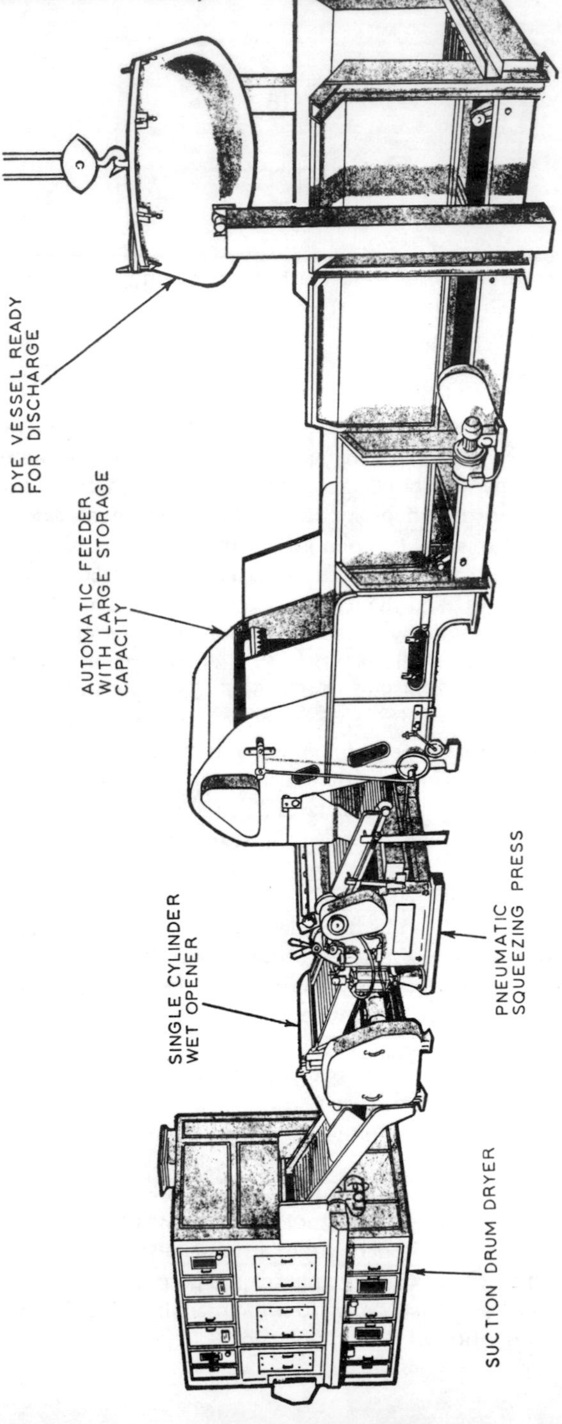

DYE VESSEL READY
FOR DISCHARGE

AUTOMATIC FEEDER
WITH LARGE STORAGE
CAPACITY

SINGLE CYLINDER
WET OPENER

PNEUMATIC
SQUEEZING PRESS

SUCTION DRUM DRYER

FIG.36 Unloading, opening and drying loose wool after dyeing.
(Petrie & McNaught Ltd)

Yarn Dyeing

Yarn may be dyed either in hanks or on specially-wound soft cheeses.

Hank dyeing is the older method and a machine for dyeing knitting yarns is shown in Plate 37. The hanks of yarn are arranged in a framework and lowered into the dye-vat. The dye-liquor is circulated through the hanks by means of a pump or impeller.

Many yarns today, however, are dyed in cheese form. The cheeses are very loosely wound and are stacked on perforated spindles, each of which holds about six cheeses. The spindles are fitted into the dyeing machine and the dye liquor is forced through them and through the cheeses of yarn. Arrangements are provided for reversing the direction of liquor flow to assist penetration.

Piece Dyeing

Woollen piece dyeing is done in a winch machine, which consists essentially of a specially-shaped stainless steel tank above which is the winch itself—a rotating reel placed above the surface of the dye liquor as shown in Fig. 37. This winch carries the piece round and round through the liquor in the form of an endless band, while the dye liquor is slowly raised to the boil and maintained at this temperature until the dyeing is finished. The dissolved colour is poured into a compartment of the tank called a *stuffing box* which allows the dye to diffuse slowly into the dyebath, and also holds the heating device so that it does not make direct contact with the cloth. Modern machines are often totally enclosed, but have windows to enable the pieces to be seen during dyeing.

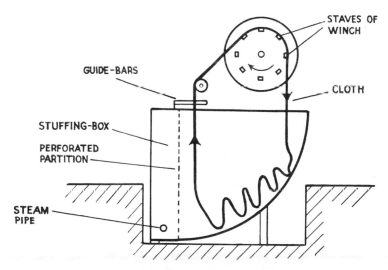

FIG.37 Side elevation of a winch for dyeing woollen pieces.

CHOICE OF METHOD OF DYEING

The range of effects obtained in piece dyeing is much smaller than is possible by weaving together yarns dyed different colours, or yarns made by mixing differently coloured fibres which have been dyed as loose wool and mixed in blending and carding. On the other hand an advantage of piece dyeing is that stocks of cloth can be held in the undyed state and quickly dyed to any shade that fashion decrees at any particular time. The shades, however, will be solids unless use is made in the fabric of effect threads such as cotton or man-made fibres which are not dyed or stained by wool dyes in the piece dyeing process, or which take the dye differently.

If mixture shades such as lovat, heather or grey are required the materials must, of course, be dyed in the loose form to the required component colours, the correct mixture-shade being obtained during blending and carding. This guarantees a more level shade in the yarn or piece than can be obtained by yarn or piece dyeing, but there is the disadvantage that the wastes made at each of the carding, spinning and twisting operations are coloured and therefore usually of less value than undyed white wastes. In addition, if small lots of different colours are processed the blending, carding and spinning machinery has to be cleaned frequently if later lots are not to be contaminated by stray fibres from a previous dyeing.

Bibliography

This list contains a limited selection of books which are currently available for purchase; additionally others will be in stock at public libraries, particularly in textile areas.

RAW MATERIALS
Wool: an Introduction to Wool Production and Marketing. H.S. Bell. (Pitman, 1970).
Handbook of Textile Fibres, Vols. 1 & 2. J.G. Cook. 4th edition. (Merrow, 1968).
Man-made Fibres. R.W. Moncrieff. 6th edition. (Newnes-Butterworth, 1975).

YARN MANUFACTURE
Woollen Carding. (Wira, 1968).
Spinning in the '70's. P.R. Lord. (Merrow, 1970).
Woollen Carding and Spinning. L. Mackereth. (Mackereth, 1975).
The Spinning Mule. H. Catling. (David & Charles, 1973).

FABRIC MANUFACTURE
Textile Design and Colour. W. Watson. 7th edition. (Newnes-Butterworth, 1975).
Positive Let-off Motions. R. Foster. (Wira, 1961).
Knitting. H. Wignall. (Pitman, 1967).
Principles of Weaving. R. Marks & A.T.C. Robinson. (Textile Institute, 1976).
Woven Cloth Construction. A.T.C. Robinson & R. Marks. (Textile Institute, 1973).

CARPET MANUFACTURE
Carpets and other Floorcoverings. G. Robinson. 2nd edition. (Textile Book Service, 1972).

DYEING AND FINISHING
Dyeing and Printing. S.R. Cockett. (Pitman, 1964).
Handbook of Textile Finishing. A.J. Hall. 3rd edition. (Iliffe, 1966).
The Theory and Practice of Wool Dyeing. C.L. Bird. 4th Edition. (Soc. Dyers & Colourists, 1972).

SCIENTIFIC ASPECTS AND TESTING
An Outline of Statistical Methods for use in the Textile Industry. A. Brearley & D.R. Cox. 9th edition (Wira, 1979)
Identification of Textile Materials. C.A. Farnfield & D.R. Perry. 7th edition. (Textile Institute, 1976).
Principles of Textile Testing. J.E. Booth. 3rd edition. (Iliffe, 1968),
Technology of Textile Properties. Marjorie A. Taylor. (Forbes, 1972).

DIRECTORIES AND GENERAL VOLUMES

Skinners British Textile Register 1975. (IPC Business Press, 1975).

How to find out about the Wool Textile Industry. Hugo Lemon. (Pergammon Press, 1968).

The British Wool Manual. Several authors. (Columbine Press, 1970).

Wool Trade—Past and Present. K.G. Ponting. (Columbine Press, 1961).

Standard Handbook of Textiles. A.J. Hall. 8th edition. (Newnes-Butterworth, 1974).

The Wira Textile Data Book. A. Rae & R. Bruce. (Wira, 1973).

The Worsted Industry. A. Brearley & J.A. Iredale. (Wira, 1980).

Textile Terms and Definitions. C.A. Farnfield & P.J. Alvie. 7th edition. (Textile Institute, 1975).

Textile Mathematics, Vols. 1, 2 & 3. J.E. Booth. (Textile Institute, 1975—77)

The situation regarding the availability for purchase of textile books is of necessity, always changing. Up-to-date information is available from professional bodies in the UK such as:

International Wool Secretariat, Valley Drive, Ilkley, W. Yorkshire, LS29 8PB.

The Society of Dyers & Colourists, PO Box 244, 82 Grattan Road, Bradford, BD1 2JB.

The Textile Institute, 10 Blackfriars Street, Manchester, M3 5DR. (Book list available.)

Wira, Wira House, West Park Ring Road, Leeds, LS16 6QL (Book list available.)

PLATE 1 (Top) Woollen yarn. (Bottom) Worsted yarn.
(International Wool Secretariat)

(a)

(b)

PLATE 2 (a) Typical woollen fabrics. (b) Typical worsted fabrics.

PLATE 3   Wool scouring bowl showing harrow-fork mechanism.

The movement of the wool is from right to left; the hopper feed is seen at the top right of the photograph, and the second bowl is at the bottom left.

(Petrie & McNaught Ltd)

PLATE 4   Petrie/Wira Improved Scouring Set.

The wool is moving from the bottom right hand corner of the photograph towards the dryer seen at the top left corner.

(Petrie & McNaught Ltd)

PLATE 5   Wool carbonizing plant.

D. Carbonizing dryer
H. Hopper-feed
W. Wool willow
C_1 & C_2. Double crushing machines

S. Shaking machine and dust extractor
N. Neutralizing bowl
R_1 & R_2. Rinse bowls
F. Final dryer

(Petrie & McNaught Ltd)

PLATE 6   Intermittent shake-willey

Sometimes referred to as a Shaker or a Teaser. The photograph shows one of the grids which extend under the swift withdrawn, as for cleaning. Before running, the machine would be adequately guarded.The feed is at the left and delivery is at the top centre of the machine at right angles to the feed.

(Haigh-Chadwick Ltd)

PLATE 7 Fearnought.

The feed sheet is on the left. The top covers are lowered and the side covers (at right) are closed when the machine is in operation.

(Haigh-Chadwick Ltd)

PLATE 8 Woollen blending.

Part of a blending department using a Spenstead Automatic Blending System.

(Spencer & Halstead Ltd)

PLATE 9   Woollen card sets for synthetics.

Feed is at the back left of the photograph; four-height series tape condensers may be seen in the centre of the picture. Waste threads are returned from condenser to hopper by an overhead suction device. In the foreground movable bobbin stands holding full condenser bobbins may be seen.
(William Tatham Ltd)

PLATE 10   Woollen carding shed.

The scribbler parts are on the right of the machines. The centre draw intermediate feed may be seen on the card in the foreground of the photograph. Notice also the safety guard over the feed sheet of the carder section (on left).
(William Tatham Ltd)

PLATE 11   A carding shed in Scotland showing ball-and-bank feeds.
Bailing machine on right (i.e. delivery from scribbler); bank on left, feeding to intermediate.

PLATE 12   Lap former.
Note machinery guards, necessary to comply with safety regulations
(William Tatham Ltd)

PLATE 13   Double ring doffer condenser.
Only the top doffer can be seen clearly.
(Haigh-Chadwick Ltd)

PLATE 14   Tandem-creel tape condenser.
Four-height, sixteen condenser bobbins, five ends per bobbin; suitable for supplying a six- or seven-inch pitch ring frame.
(Haigh-Chadwick Ltd)

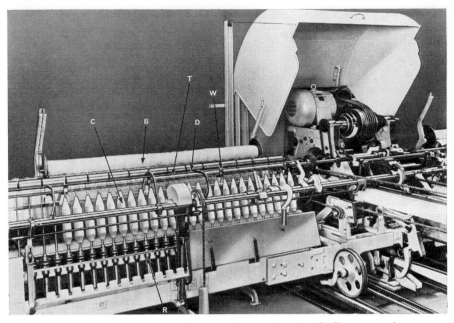

PLATE 15(a)   High speed woollen mule, electrically operated.

B. Condenser bobbins holding slubbing
C. Cops of yarn
D. Delivery Rollers.

R. Rabbeth spindles (high speed, roller bearings)
T. Counter faller
W. Winding faller

(Wilson & Longbottom Ltd)

PLATE 15(b)   Woollen mules.

The condenser bobbins are seen on the right; carriage holding cops of spun yarn is on the left.
(Halifax Courier Ltd)

PLATE 16
The passage of material from condenser bobbins to the spindles on a woollen ring frame (MWR5).

Single balloon control rings surround the yarn packages. The frame has two lines of condenser bobbins (see Plate 17)—all the slubbing ends from a bobbin pass to the spindles on the same side of the frame. A row of empty packages is seen in front of the spindles in readiness for doffing. Note also the broken-end collectors (working by suction), i.e. nozzles, which may be seen beneath the front rollers.

(Platt Saco Lowell Ltd)

PLATE 17 Woollen ring spinning frames (MWR5).
Note the variable speed motors and the dials for indicating speed.
(Platt Saco Lowell Ltd)

PLATE 18
Ring doubling frame.

Note the end detectors behind the delivery rollers (only one in use) and the balloon control rings.
(Platt Saco Lowell Ltd)

PLATE 19
Cone winding.

Supply packages are seen in the foreground; wound cones are at the back of the machine.
(W. Schlafhorst & Co.
UK agent: BL Engineering Ltd)

PLATE 20 Reeling machine.
(Croon Lucke Maschinenfabrik GmbH & Co. UK agent: F. Uttley & Sons Ltd)

PLATE 21
Pirn winding.

One unit (four spindles) of a fully automatic pirn winding machine. The spindles and partially filled pirns are horizontal on the left of the machine, empty packages on the right. The supply bobbins are seen upright at the rear of the unit.
(Hacoba Textilmaschinen. UK agent: Crowther Ltd)

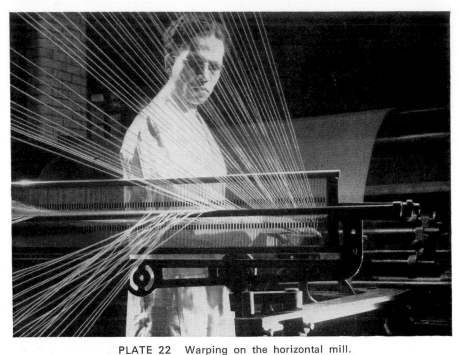

PLATE 22 Warping on the horizontal mill.

The threads are seen passing through the leasing reed (see Fig. 23(a)); the balloon of yarn on the mill is in the background.

(International Wool Secretariat)

PLATE 23 A set of yarn scouring machines suitable for woollen yarn.

The tapes which carry the skeins of yarn through the four scouring bowls can be seen.
(Petrie & McNaught Ltd)

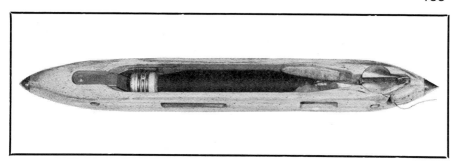

PLATE 24   Shuttle with Northrop weft-bobbin for automatic weaving.
(British Northrop Ltd)

PLATE 25   Tappet loom.

T. Tappets		H. Healds and reed
O. Over-pick	P. Picker	M. Take-up motion

PLATE 26   Hattersley 'Standard' loom with positive V-dobby.

B. Shuttle-boxes (four at each side)
C. Cloth roller
T. Take-up roller
D. Lever-dobby
J. Jack-levers
H. Healds
U. Picking-stick (underpick)

Several different versions of this loom are made.

PLATE 27   Dobcross HK 4 x 4 box loom for weaving up to seven colours.

Also made as a 4 x 1 fully automatic loom with up to four colours (but not in single picks). Speed up to 130ppm. Reed spaces from 130—460cm (50—180in.); standard width 230cm (90in) to produce 210-cm (82-in) fabric which will be finished to about 145cm (56in). Overall pick range: 10—246 picks per inch. Positive let-off. Take-up with chain and spur-wheel drive, and worm-and-wheel drive to 'grater' roller. Up to 30-in diameter beam flange.

B. Shuttle boxes   H. Healds   T. Temples   W. Wheel dobby

PLATE 28
Jacquard on Northrop loom.

PLATE 29
Sulzer six-colour weaving
machine type 85 SSD-KR.

Maximum reed space of 220cm
(87in.); Stäubli rotary dobby with
the colour change controlled by
the dobby. Maximum weft
insertion rate 540 metres per
minute and 250 picks per minute.
Note creel of cones is on left,
roll of woven fabric at front of
machine.

PLATE 30   Rapier loom.
The dobby may be seen on the left, above the loom.
(SACM. UK agent: BL Engineering Ltd)

PLATE 31   Northrop automatic loom, F-model 4-box.
B.   Bobbins of weft ready for manual loading into magazine   C.   Bobbin-changing mechanism
D.   Dobby   E.   Container to collect empty weft bobbins ejected from shuttle
M.   Magazine or battery of full weft bobbins
The loom has a positive worm let-off motion, a Northrop centre weft-fork motion and a positive
continuous worm take-up motion.
(British Northrop Ltd)

PLATE 32 Hattersley automatic blanket loom.
The loom has a positive cam-treading motion (bottom teft).

PLATE 33   Tentering machine.
(E. Gordon Whiteley Ltd)

PLATE 34 Cloth raising.
(Wilson & Longbottom Ltd)

PLATE 35 Dry finishing department.
Cutting (cropping or shearing) machines are seen on the left and right foreground. The flock
collection and removal is by means of overhead trunking.

PLATE 36   Blowing machine.
(James Bailey (Engineers) Ltd)

PLATE 37   Longclose hank-dyeing machines.

Some things are designed to do work out of all proportion to their size.

, Occupying only two square metres, the Repco SELFIL spinner is one of the smallest yarn spinners ever made.

Yet it produces almost 3 kg of 34 metric count yarn per hour at 300 metres per minute.

One operator can look after 8-12 machines; what's more they will be happy to do so thanks to SELFIL's clean, quiet and simple operation.

A 2 hp driving motor and a 0.5 hp suction unit keep power consumption amazingly low.

Which altogether means a great deal more yarn for a great deal less floor space, labour and power.

SELFIL produces unique singles-type spun yarns which comprise a single strand of staple fibres reinforced by two synthetic continuous filaments.

Because these unique, completely torque-balanced yarns have high strength and low fault rates, high knitting efficiencies can be achieved in top class fabrics.

SELFIL fabrics have high abrasion resistance. They're free from bagging and sagging, and are particularly resistant to pilling.

Finally, the SELFIL, incorporating all its unique design and production features, represents a major development in textile engineering.

Write for details.

Platt Saco Lowell

Marketing PO Box 55 Accrington BB5 0RN Lancashire England
Telephone Accrington (0254) 382101 Telex 63447 Cables Platsaco Accrington
A division of Stone-Platt Industries Ltd

10749

142

HAIGH-CHADWICK LIMITED

TEXTILE
MACHINE MAKERS

Manufacturers of:

OPENING MACHINERY,

WORSTED CARDING MACHINERY,

SLIVER, NON-WOVEN AND COMPACT CARDS,

WOOLLEN CARDING MACHINERY,

WOOLLEN SPINNING FRAMES

HAIGH-CHADWICK LIMITED

TELEX
517291

MARSH MILLS, CLECKHEATON
WEST YORKSHIRE BD19 5BQ.,
ENGLAND

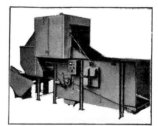

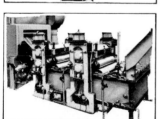

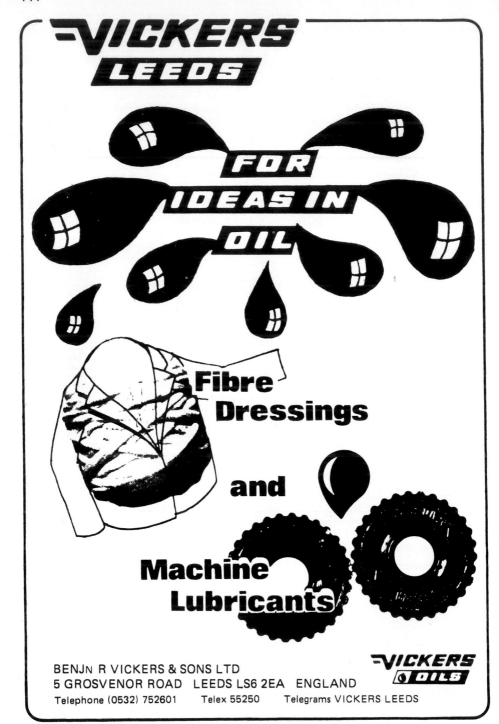

how's this
for two-upmanship

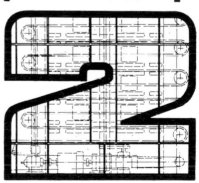

MECHANICALLY...

The EGW 'Velset' or 'Velocitair' multi-layer drying/heating setting machine

(1) Uses minimum floor space for a given production
(2) Has modular construction to suit production requirements
(3) Is constructed with easy maintenance in mind
(4) Can be designed to specific requirements

Please write for fuller details.

FABRIC WISE...

The EGW 'Velset' or 'Velocitair' machine

(1) Has provision for heat setting
(2) Dries wide range of fabrics at maximum speeds
(3) Processes from heaviest felts to light weight suitings
(4) Has continuous operation

EGW **E. Gordon Whiteley Ltd**
Beech Works, Morley, Leeds LS27 ONL, England
Cables: Tentering Morley; Telex: 557460

The Thorn way to process and quality control

Thorn Automation's quality control and process monitoring equipment is playing an important part in the textile industry at many stages from fibre and yarn processing through to knitting and weaving.

Thorn equipment not only improves quality but also increases productivity in the wollen industry.

The Autocount measures, records and controls woollen and fibre slubbings continuously on the machine.

The Thorn Mk 2 yarn clearer clears slubs, doubled yarn and third ends in 2 fold yarn. Humidity, moisture regain, conductive yarns or colour variations present no problem with a Thorn yarn clearer. And there are many other features too.

Other well proven quality control instruments available from Thorn Automation for use in the process or laboratory include the WIRA yarn tension meter, WIRA warp tension meter, WIRA fibre fineness meter, WIRA single fibre strength meter, and the WIRA rapid oil extraction apparatus.

Get in touch with us today and we will see you get full information.

THORN AUTOMATION

Thorn Automation Limited
Beech Avenue, New Basford,
Nottingham NG7 7JJ
Telephone 0602 76123
Telex 37142

Control instruments and equipment for the textile industry.

Index

Page numbers in brackets refer to the Plates.